CW00455258

Leslie Beaton-Brown

Leslie Beaton-Brown
MY LIFE IN PROPERTY

ISBN 9781077459236

Publishing services provided by www.simonweir.co.uk

For Linda and my children, as requested

Contents

Leslie Beaton-Brown

Foreword

There are plenty of stories about successful business people, but very few about people who have come from a background of no family money and a limited wartime education. It takes an exceptional individual to go from such a start to being a huge success in the property business. That is my father's story.

Walt Disney liked to say that his success was built on the four Cs: curiosity; confidence; courage; and constancy. Leslie's story is one of success as well – and shows that he was always curious, even as a boy. His confidence never waivered and his courage is clear, seen in the bold business decisions taken in his constant pursuit of a property empire.

I've often wondered how someone with so much humility could become so dedicated to achieving respect and recognition. Leslie's story shows how this happened naturally over the years, with the directions he mapped out and the people he chose to have around him, motivating them with the vision he held so strongly and, of course, with sheer sweat, determination and hard work.

While his story is mostly of a business nature, you can rest assured that Leslie has always been motivated by his deep love for his family. He shows how having strong family ethics, coupled with 100% belief and imagination, breeds success and he has never stopped trying to make life better for his family. My father's story also clearly shows that you make your own luck in life, when you take the opportunities presented to you. It also shows how important people can be, because certain key people shaped Leslie's path and enabled him to flourish. Life is a journey and there is no doubt that he has enjoyed his.

I'm grateful for these and all the lessons Leslie has taught us all. I'm very proud and eternally grateful to be able to call him my dad.

Sarah Beretta, 2019

Chapter One

Foundations

Property development may have become my professional life, but property was not initially in my blood. I was not born into a wealthy family with land and money behind me. My father – James Edward Beaton-Brown – was born on April 5, 1898 and grew up in Archway in North London. He volunteered for the army at the outbreak of the First World War, though in 1914 he would have been just 16 years old. After training he enlisted in the Duke of Cambridge's Own (Middlesex Regiment), Second Battalion, and shipped out to fight for his country.

The Middlesex Regiment, nicknamed the Die Hards, took part in some of the bloodiest battles of the war – from the Battle of Albert and the early stages of the Battle of the Somme to the Second Battle of Ypres, which was the first time the Germans used gas on the battlefield, continuing all the way to the Armistice. From August 1914 until the end of the war four years later, Middlesex battalions fought in 81 battles, won five Victoria Crosses and lost more than12,000 men.

James was one of the fortunate ones who survived, though he saw action around the Belgian towns of Ypres and Passchendaele and

Meet the family: my father James Beaton-Brown with his parents, some time after 1900

elsewhere. And he *was* lucky – I have his army identification tag (pictured, left), a circle of brass an inch across, folded nearly in half where it stopped a German bullet. That disc may well have saved his life. My father would tell the story of how, at the height of one front-line skirmish, he dived into a deep trench full of water to avoid heavy German machine-gun fire. The trouble was, the water was much deeper than it had looked and James – being a non-swimmer – was in real danger of drowning. Fortunately for him, two of his mates in the battalion had also dived in and they got to him just in time to keep him afloat.

My father didn't escape the trenches entirely unharmed, though. After several months on the front line he was wounded and taken back to England to recuperate. It must have been around this time that he met Marion Maude Elliot and, after a short courtship, they were married on October 24, 1917. James was 19 and Marion was 20.

Fortune smiled on him again, in that he wasn't returned to the Western Front. Instead he was seconded to the British expeditionary force that was being sent to Russia, to link up with White Russian forces resisting the revolutionaries. The aim of the British mission was to rescue the Tsar and his family, but it was too late: the Russian royal family was executed on July 17, 1918 in Ekatrinburg, while my

My parents, Marion and James Beaton-Brown

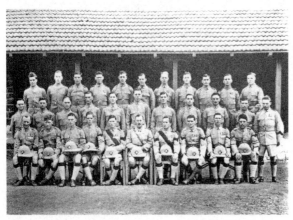

father and the rest of the rescue force was still en route to Russia.

The First World War ended with the Armistice of November 11, 1918 and the surrender of Germany, but while the Middlesex Regiment shrank dramatically from its wartime size, my father remained in service. After the war, the Die Hards were sent overseas, to garrison distant parts of the British Empire so in 1922 my parents and their young family – my brother Reggie and sisters Edna and Elsie – took the train from London down to Southampton to board a liner bound for the far side of the world.

My father sent this souvenir box from Ypres to his parents

The voyage took several weeks, the ship stopping in Istanbul, Aden (Yemen), Singapore and Ceylon (Sri Lanka) before the family finally disembarked in south-west India at the port of Madras (now called Chennai). The family moved from army camp to army camp before finally settling in married quarters at Kamptee, near the town of Nagpur in India's Central Provinces. This is where I was born on April 6, 1934.

Life for members of the British Raj in India in the 1920s and 30s was good. Even those of lower rank in the army could afford to employ a cook

My father's company in India. He's seated in the front row, second from the right

and other servants. My father had been promoted to staff sergeant and the family was comfortably settled – until my siblings were enrolled in Lovedale, a prestigious boarding school in the cool of the hill country. This, I am told, did not

My parents in India. Am I the child? I'm not sure

please them one bit, as they had to leave behind a menagerie of pets – not only a cat and a dog but also parrots (including a talking African Grey) and Jimmie, my brother's pet mongoose.

I was too young to remember this, of course. I was barely two when in 1936, after almost 15 years in India, the battalion was recalled to England. The family packed up… but left Reggie, who was just 16 years old and enrolled in the Army Cadet Force. The train journey from Southampton to Waterloo on a dark, wet winters day was an eye-opening shock for my sisters. As the train rattled through the south London suburbs, the sight of rows of drab terraces filled them with foreboding – it was a vision that was to stay with them all their lives.

As we looked likely to be based in England, my father bought a small house on the outskirts of East Dagenham in Essex – which wasn't a suburb of London as it is today but surrounded by open countryside. It wasn't a grand house by any means, but it was big enough for our small family, especially once my eldest sister Edna left to set up her own home. In India she had met a young sergeant of the Shropshire Light Infantry called Tim Holding and they'd stayed in touch, even after we returned to England. When his regiment was recalled to Shropshire as tensions with Germany escalated, Edna went to join him. They were married in Shrewsbury on June 6, 1939 – just before the outbreak of the Second World War.

The second war with Germany saw the British Army swell in size again. My father was still in service and, as an experienced soldier and veteran of the First World War, he was promoted to the rank of captain. However, he was too old for further front-line action and became instead the adjutant-in-charge of the large camp built to hold German and Italian prisoners of war at Wormwood Scrubs, near Shepherd's Bush in West London.

Edna's husband Tim had a distinguished career in the war, serving in North Africa and the Middle East, rising to the rank of major and finally being appointed Town Mayor of Cairo. My other sister

My father in the Second World War

Elsie had also married. Her husband was a local man, Sam Dean, was a sergeant in the Royal Marines. He was on *HMS Ark Royal* when it was attacked by German U-boats and aircraft.

Meanwhile Reggie, out in India, was also caught up in the war. After the Army Cadet Force, he had enlisted with the York & Lancaster Light Infantry. The Japanese entered the war in 1941 and swept across Asia, beginning a major assault on British territory in Burma, heading for India. Fighting was fierce and British forces were hard pressed to hold them off. One senior British officer came up with a bold strategy to take them on. In 1942 Brigadier Orde Wingate set up the Long Range

My brother Reggie and his wife Madge on their wedding day

My brother Reggie, a sergeant in the Yorkshire & Lancashire regiment. On his arm is the badge of Wingate's Chindits

Penetration Group – which became known as Wingate's Chindits. They marched into the Burmese jungle, supplied by air drops of equipment and rations. They began attacking military supply lines deep in Japanese territory. I'm proud to say that Reggie was part of it.

I was just a child attending the local junior school when the war broke out, but even I was deeply caught up in it. Once the Luftwaffe began bombing London and other cities, the government decided to evacuate children to the safety of the countryside. We were all provided with gas masks and I vividly remember clutching my small case tightly in my hand, boarding a coach filled with children from all over London. I was only seven years old at the time.

It was a long journey, jolting around on the coach – this was before the days of motorways, of course. I'm sure some of the children on the bus would have cried at the start of it, but I can't honestly tell you if I was one of them. We were taken to a small village called Langford in Somerset, more than 170 miles from my home in Dagenham.

It was early evening when we got off the coach at the village hall, where a large group of adults was waiting. I understand now they were people who'd volunteered to take in the evacuees. We stood in the hall and people would come up and say, "I'll take that one", as if picking up the shopping. I left with another boy my age, Martin from Haringey. We'd been selected by a young, recently married couple called the Bristows. They took us to their

15

home, a short walk away on the edge of the village overlooking fields and farmland. They were wonderful, caring surrogate parents and I settled in quickly – though naturally I missed my own parents.

Mum and dad did come to visit me after I'd been in Langford for a few months, though the trip was nearly a disaster. As their train was pulling into Bristol, it had to stop in the long approach tunnel before the station as wave after wave of German bombers pounded the city. Fortunately, the tunnel wasn't hit and the railway wasn't

The Bristows, who took me in when I was evacuated to Somerset in the war

damaged, but it did delay my parents – who didn't arrive until the next day. Martin's mother also came to visit him. Twice, in fact – and on the second time she took him back to Haringey. I can't say I missed him.

My three-and-a-half years with the Bristows was fairly idyllic. Mrs Bristow's parents owned a farm, which we visited frequently. It was a real treat for me to feed the chickens and ducks that roamed freely around the farmyard and see the milking parlour in full swing. This was an old-fashioned parlour, with the cows milked by hand. I tried it, of course, but I wasn't a natural at it. All in all, it was a very happy time for me and I believe it planted a deep-seated desire in me for a country life, which I later fulfilled when buying an estate in Scotland.

But my time in Somerset did come to an end as Mrs Bristow was expecting her first child. I returned to Dagenham in 1943, with the war still in full swing. I enrolled in the Park Secondary School where, I must confess, I was an average pupil academically. Fortunately, I excelled at sports – cricket, athletics and football. I was an early riser in those days and would often be out of the house by 6am, enjoying the countryside around Dagenham, collecting mushrooms or scrumping apples, plums and greengages (a particular favourite of my mother) from the local orchards. They were wonderful, carefree days.

Of course, the war was still very much going on and I remember seeing dogfights between German aircraft and allied fighter squadrons based in nearby Hornchurch. There were American army bases all over East Anglia, with convoys of trucks passing through Dagenham. These were of great interest to us local children, as the Yanks would throw handfuls of sweets to us from the windows of their lorries. Any time we saw them approaching, we'd run to the side of the road and shout, "Got any gum, chum?" Sure enough, handfuls of goodies would land at our feet.

London was still very much under attack from the air at this time. I must have seen dozens of the V1 rockets – the Doodlebugs – as they passed over Essex, aimed indescriminately at the city. They'd pass overhead with a distinctive *pop-pop-pop* sound... which was normal, because when the engine went quiet they would glide to earth and and that's when they wrought vast damage.

Me as an evacuee (government-issue gas mask not pictured)

It was in 1944 that Reggie came to England on leave. I was excited to meet him – I'd been so young when we left India that I didn't really remember him at all. Unfortunately, he arrived suffering from malaria so was bed-ridden for weeks. No doubt it was the age gap, but I must sadly confess that he remained a complete stranger to me – even after the war. While waiting to be fitted for his demob suit Reggie met a lovely girl called

Madge, who he went on to marry – settling near her family in Derby. After growing up in India my brother had little affinity for England and could not come to terms with the cold winter weather in the north. Within a few months, he and Madge emigrated to Perth in Western Australia.

An early photograph of me

The war ended in 1945 and, shortly after that, my father's commission ended too. He'd been in the army his entire adult life, so what was he to do? The answer was the Women's Voluntary Service, which offered him a management position that came with a flat in their Cadogan Square headquarters in central London. Moving from Dagenham to the heart of the city on a grey winter's day was devastating for a country boy like me. I was miserable and couldn't settle in the new surroundings. My parents even took me to see a doctor, they were so concerned about my health.

I attended the Cook's Ground School, off the King's Road in Chelsea and things began to improve for me. I began to make friends, they put me straight into the first team for football – and I started watching Chelsea FC at Stamford Bridge, who I've supported all my life. I did reasonably well at this school and stayed there even when my parents left the WVS to work for a businessman called John Spencer. We moved into his grand house at Queen Anne Street in the West End and that's where I was when I left school at 16 years old. Though he couldn't have guessed where it would eventually lead, it was Mr Spencer who got me started in property. He arranged for me to attend an interview with Amery Underwood, chairman of Hampton & Sons, a large firm of Estate Agents in Arlington Street, opposite The Ritz Hotel. That was the beginning of my career.

Chapter Two
The Apprenticeship

Istarted work at Hamptons & Sons in the summer of 1950.. I was a typical 16-year-old and life in the accounts department was not to my taste – adding up columns of figures wasn't my forte and even the £2.50 a week salary couldn't stop me becoming bored and restless. However, around this time I met a young woman, Patricia, and as can happen with young people, she became pregnant. I married her and the need to provide for my young family kept me working doggedly for 18 months or so.

I wasn't happy in accounts, though. I was addressing envelopes and doing all the other menial jobs juniors always do. Hamptons were managing agents for many blocks of flats and when the rents came in, I'd have to walk round the West End – it always seemed to be piddling with rain when I was doing it – banking the cheques in various different branches. I knew it wasn't for me – this wasn't my life. So when I unexpectedly heard that Len Harvey, the senior industrial property manager, needed a junior assistant I made a point of contacting him and expressing my interest. We got on well in the interview and I started working for him the following Monday, with the blessing of Jimmy Rae, the firm's head accountant.

Len Harvey was a chartered surveyor, a mature man. Naturally as I was the junior, I was doing all the jobs he was too busy to do himself. But this wasn't like the drudgery of the accounts department and from the very beginning, I took to this new role with enthusiasm.

Mr Harvey – as I addressed him in those days – had me ringing up firms enquiring about property, getting the details, doing the legwork for him. I remember our first deal was 225 Lea Bridge Road in Leyton, one of the less glamorous parts of London's East End. It was a single-storey factory of about 5000sq-ft occupied by the Holmes Brothers. We put a board on that factory and the number of phone calls it generated was unbelievable – most of the phone calls were delegated to me and I remember a particular enquiry from Salini Brothers, who made the most attractive decorative smoking pipes – the kind of article you see in the Dunhill shop in Jermyn Street. They didn't take this building, though we eventually sold them another factory. We did, however, sell the Lea Bridge Road premises fairly quickly – and I was hooked.

I became committed to the job. It was interesting, exciting and Len Harvey was a kind man and I enjoyed working for him. I remember he gave me five pounds one Christmas as a present – which was a lot of money in those days; I could have gone on holiday to the South of France on that.

While I was working with him at Hamptons, Len Harvey suffered a terrible accident in his garden. Bending down, he got a pea-stick in the eye and lost it. Though he eventually got a glass eye, he wore an eyepatch for much of the time I was there. He was a good man, always free with his advice and expertise. We stayed in touch even after I left Hamptons – he'd call me up sometimes, when I was much more successful, and say "I see you did a deal on such-and-such a property; I'd had that enquiry but I couldn't place it."

In my early days working with Mr Harvey, I didn't have any idea how important the other people in Business Premises Department would be to me in later years – one person in particular, who sat at the desk opposite me. Harry Hyams was a brilliant young negotiator. By

Giving my sister Edna a lift. I was at Hamptons when I bought that blazer

the time he was 25, he'd already made several million through property developments jointly undertaken with entrepreneurs Felix Fenston, Jack Rose, Joe Levy and others. He made a real impression on me – young, smart, well-dressed and successful.

Harry
Hyams

I would often stay late in the offices and it was common for Mr Hyams to drop in to pick up a document or check his messages, on his way to some engagement in the West End. "You're working late, Leslie," he'd say – and I'd take the opportunity to ask him about his latest deals or ask him about the bases for valuation, yields and other elements of the business I didn't understand at the time. He'd always patiently offer me an explanation in his own way, making sure I understood the basics.

I was enjoying my job immensely and had already three and a half successful years with Hamptons, when Harry Hyams spoke to me one evening and said he wanted me to see a friend of his. He gave me a name and a phone number, but said nothing else. Intrigued, I called the number and arranged to visit Harry's friend Jack Goldhill at his New Cavendish Street office. He was a partner in Leighton Goldhill Estate Agents, who were preparing to move to larger premises in New Bond Street – where they wanted to establish an Industrial Property department. Harry Hyams had recommended me for the position… would I be interested?

Well, I was and I agreed to start when they moved into the new offices. When I handed in my notice at Hamptons, they offered me an increase in salary to £6 a week plus my own day book – which meant I would receive a commission on any transaction I did. But I wasn't going to pass up this new opportunity – especially as the introduction had come from Harry Hyams. And besides, Jack Goldhill was going to pay me £15 a week, plus 12.5% commission on every deal I did.

When I arrived in New Bond Street I found that Leighton Goldhill didn't actually have any instructions or even any enquiries for industrial property. I was starting with a completely blank sheet of paper.

Sadly, my marriage to Pat was falling apart – inevitably as we had been far too young when we married. Our characters and backgrounds were streets apart and we wanted different things from life. Even though we had children – my eldest daughter Gaile and twins Garry and Denise – we had grown so far apart that it was a relief for both of us when we separated and then divorced. To be honest, I reproach myself now for leaving Pat with three young children, but I have always remained in constant touch with them and have provided for them throughout their lives.

I threw myself into my new job. I remember the first deal I did: within my first month, I let a building in Acton to Coventry Climax Engines Limited. At that time, there were really only four big players in industrial property in the London area: Brixton Estates; Percy Bilton; Slough Estates; and Allnat London Properties. I'd managed to get friendly with Mr Pratt, one of the directors of Allnat. So when I noticed an advert from Coventry Climax Engines requiring property in the Acton area, I called him up. Did he have anything?

"As it happens, we've just bought premises in Acre Lane," he told me. I quickly called the clients, arranged for their representative to meet Mr Pratt at the property in the morning and a deal was agreed. That's how industry worked in those days: companies needed space and deals were done quickly. Of course, after that I had Mr Pratt's ear.

The success of that first deal owed as much to the luck of timing as spotting the opportunity. This was a key part of the business. Drinks-manufacturer Britvic had sent a circular round to all the agents: "wanted, distribution premises in the Wembley or Perivale area". Again, I phoned Mr Pratt to see if he had something suitable. He explained that the Ministry of Works had seconded a number of the buildings on the Perivale Industrial Estate for war-effort use and they were shortly to release back one large building in Water Road… and these were great, modern buildings. I quickly called Britvic and we arranged to meet at the property the following week.

At this time, Britvic was an American-owned company and it was expanding rapidly in the UK. As Mr Pratt and I waited outside the

Perivale site, we saw the Britvic executive arrive in a chauffeur-driven Cadillac. We walked around the property and he was clearly interested. When he enquired about the rental terms, Mr Pratt said something like £15,000 a year – high for the times, but Britvic agreed to take it. "But I've never heard of your company," said Mr Pratt. "I'll have to check your references." The man from Britvic didn't blink. "Don't worry, Mr Pratt," he replied. "I'll have my bank manager contact you. You'll see we're more than able to meet your terms."

After that deal, I had several other agents who used to deal with Allnat ringing me up to complain. One even said, "You're ruining the market! The rents you've achieved are out of all proportion to value." But I wasn't asking for the rent. My role was simply to provide customers who were prepared to pay the terms quoted.

That Britvic deal was my first really big contract and it landed me my first big commission. I remember Richard Leighton, Jack Goldhill's partner, taking me aside to counsel me: "That's an awful lot of money, Leslie… you really have to be careful to look after it."

They were good years at Leighton Goldhill. I was earning a serious wage as a negotiator and industry was expanding, with an insatiable demand for warehousing and factory space – which meant I was always busy. My personal life settled down as well, as I went from going to the cinema and having dinner with Barbara, one of the secretaries at Leighton Goldhill, to becoming more serious and we married in 1959, with our reception in the Café Royal in Regent's Street and our honeymoon in the Caribbean.

Even so, in 1962 a chance meeting with another agent opened a new professional opportunity for me. He knew of a small-time developer looking for someone to help move the business forward – and the way he described it intrigued me. I went to see them and they had big ideas, even though they might not have had the finance to get into the big league – but they had enough to get started. We got on well and they offered me the position. Jack Goldhill was disappointed when I gave him my notice, especially as we'd become good friends, but he wished me luck.

Chapter Three

From employee to owner

When I joined Felix & Partners, it became immediately clear that Armand Felix was not a property man. He had a bit of capital to help get schemes going but his partner Tommy Pike was experienced and had been in property all his life. It was Mr Pike who'd bought me into the business – and he was more than delighted that I was going to work with them in Wigmore Street, where they had rented offices in Wigmore Hall.

I was in my early twenties and Tommy Pike would have been over 50 and he taught me a great deal. He had an old Rolls Royce and we drove around England, looking at sites in every corner of the country. Bearing in mind that British Industry was actively looking for premises or sites for expansion, we were getting more and more serious enquiries.

The first major deal I did with Felix & Partners was in Worcester – a centre for raw-food products, but the whole area had major problems with flooding from the River Severn. I found a safe site on the outskirts of the city and oversaw the construction of a 60,000sq-ft manufacturing unit for the Chicago-based conglomerate Armour & Co, big players in the food-canning and baked-beans industry, and we agreed terms to sell (rather than lease) the premises to them on completion.

I went to Felix & Partners as an employee – but my letter of appointment from Armand Felix gave me a third of all profit in any developments I introduced the company. This was to prove greatly to my advantage later. I attended lots of meetings with Tommy Pike with various companies and I was learning a great deal from him. However, it wasn't long before I was definitely making a major contribution to the business: while Mr Pike had the technical property knowledge, he didn't have the drive that I did. It got to the stage that I had more work going on under my third-share of the business than the other two put together. When I started, they had just one development and Armand Felix never introduced anything – he was purely a man there with a couple of hundred thousand pounds to get things going.

In 1962, we were developing a site at Guildhall Street in Preston – a site that I'd found, which we'd bought for less than £2000. I could not believe how cheap it was. We got consent and started erecting an office building on spec. Before construction was even completed, we agreed to let the whole property to the Commercial Union Assurance Company.

As this project was underway, Tommy Pike took me to one side and said, "Why don't you transfer your shares in that development to me? If we're going to go forward." I couldn't quite believe it. I just looked at him and said, "What are you talking about? That's not how this works." Ironically, we sold the building on completion to our tenant Commercial Union – and I kept my third share of the profit.

Our building on Guildhall Street in Preston – sold to Commercial Union

So at that point Tommy Pike decided to get out. I think he was a bit restless, frankly. He could see that Armand Felix was never going to produce anything to expand the company and I was going to share in nearly everything that was coming along. He approached both me and Armand Felix about selling his shares, but Mr Felix didn't want to buy him out and I certainly didn't have the capital to do so. We were stuck in an unsatisfactory stalemate – so I approached Ted Woodward, my bank manager at the

Hammersmith branch of Nat West. A little to my surprise, he agreed to loan me the money to buy Mr Pike's shares. He left Felix & Partners on amicable terms, which left me owning two-thirds of the company.

I now set about expanding the business as rapidly as possible. Of course, I couldn't cope with the sheer volume of journeys and work personally, so I employed an acquaintance called Bernard Tracey, who did not have any development experience, though he had formerly worked for a firm of estate agents, Marcus Levy & Co. He came on board as a negotiator, but soon picked up the pieces and started to learn the basics of the business and started generating sites.

To be honest, Bernard had a personality I didn't have. For instance, he went to Manchester and made good contacts with people in the planning department – he got on so well with them, we were serious contenders for quite a few sites. We didn't get anything cheaper, but we did get the opportunity. And that's how business operated: you just needed the opening; take advantage of it and you're there with a sporting chance.

We had also privately agreed to purchase three city-centre sites in Manchester plus an important site in Churchgate, Bolton – which involved the purchase of two theatres, a cinema and a row of houses. There was also a 5000sq-ft warehouse off the Penworth Road in Cardiff and a much larger scheme in Guildhall Street, Preston where we had consent to erect an office building of 20,000sq-ft. Our solicitors were slowly working on the legalities, we had architects producing drawings and my quantity surveyor Roy Kinsler had negotiated building contracts with various suppliers. On that basis, we were ready to proceed… but we still hadn't actually acquired the land. We'd gone as far as we could go on a total speculative basis. But even with all the work everyone had already put in, if we didn't secure the land everything could still have evaporated. Everyone would just have said, 'bad luck' and then search |for something else.

In the early days we'd been relying on Mr Felix to provide sufficient funds for our developments, but now we'd reached his financial limit. There was no way he could put up the money for the amount of land we were looking at. It was clear that future growth could come only if we obtained a large injection of capital from the City. I began talking to the larger estate agents and financial institutions, with many a blank meeting that ended with a, "We'll let you know…" and I'd never hear another word. I was getting nowhere and needed a stroke of luck. That came in the shape of a chance meeting in The Guinea public house on Bruton Place, just off Berkeley Square.

I'd popped into the pub for a bite to eat and, as you do in busy pubs sometimes, ended up sharing a table with an older gentleman. Making polite conversation, he asked what I did and I told him I was in commercial property. "I have a friend who runs John D Wood & Co," he said. "Would you like to meet him?" Yes, I replied: "As it happens, I have several projects that might be of interest to some of his clients." We exchanged business cards and went our separate ways… and I genuinely expected to hear nothing further. That same afternoon I received a call from the partner at John D Wood and we discussed in general terms the location of the developments, the finance required and he suggested a meeting PDQ, as he was off on holiday in a few days.

We met next morning and I presented all the plans and financial appraisals – which he immediately had delivered by messenger to his client in the City. He didn't volunteer the name of his clients and I didn't frankly have a clue who they might be at the time, anyway. However, I can now say that these events totally transformed the business.

SG Warburg & Co is one of the blue-blood private banks in the City of London. I'd heard the name, of course, but simply didn't appreciate how powerful they were. I was summoned to a meeting in their Gresham Street offices to see their managing director, Frank Smith. He was an incredibly astute man – a doyen of the Square Mile. He asked me lots of questions – including a bit about myself, because you have to remember I was about 27 or 28 years old at this time and there I was, asking for backing of a few million pounds. Eventually he just said, "That's fine. Can you attend another meeting?" Of course, I replied – at any time, I'll drop anything to be there.

Architects's perspective of our development oppersite Alperton tube station

A few days later I had a phone call from another senior man at
Warburgs, called Robin Jessel. Now, the Jessel family and the Straker-
Smiths had significant involvements in Warburgs. He summoned me to a
further meeting with Frank Smith, who was very hard on me at first – but
of course I understood, they didn't want to commit large amounts of
money to an amateur. Eventually he announced that Warburgs were
seriously considering going ahead but they were thinking of a joint
venture for the finance, between themselves and the Church
Commissioners for England – did I have any objections? Well, you can
imagine I didn't have any possible objections…

Unbeknownst to me, Warburgs had already discussed my
developments directly with the Commissioners for the Church of
England. At that time, they had a fund of about £30-40 million they
wanted to invest in commercial property… but they couldn't get involved
directly – they could only fund property people and take an equity stake.
And here I was, standing in front of Warburgs, asking them to finance
the development of a commercial and industrial property portfolio
running into several million pounds.

I went to meet Donald Collinette and John Millard-Barnes of the

Commissioners, who were based at 1 Millbank in those days. If you were there at 12 o'clock, you were entitled to a glass of sherry – so they'd always time their meetings for half past eleven or so. With Warburgs and the Church Commissioners we formed an investment vehicle, Commercial Holdings Ltd, to purchase the sites and place the construction contracts. I was managing director, with Robin Jessel as company secretary, Frank Smith and Donald Collinette as directors and our independent chairman Robin van Hee was appointed, who was also a director of the Friends Provident Insurance Company. Board meetings were always held at Millbank and it was a huge step for me: from being an independent but growing developer to being managing director of a board packed with City grandees – before I was 30, as well.

On completion of construction, neary all the buildings were let (and in due course several were acquired outright by the Church Commissioners for their main in-house investment fund).

I then set about finding additional development projects. British business was booming: Goodyear, Avon, Dunlop and many other companies were all expanding and urgently required further distribution depots around the country – preferably on long-lease rental terms. This demand created a golden opportunity for a sizeable development

New depot outlet for the Avon Rubber Company, Back Road, Bristol

programme with little or no risk. For example, if the Avon Rubber Company informed us they required a depot outlet in, say, Gateshead, we would make a detailed search of the area to find a suitable site in a location approved by them and agree basic rental terms. Our development would ideally then include two or three other units on the site speculatively – and the demand for them was there.

Chapter 4

The EPIC years

I **was constantly looking for** other opportunities to grow the company but property development always involves significant amounts of capital. Even though the business was successful, I found dealing with the main clearing banks was hard work. It would always involve endless meetings before finally producing an offer of some sort of facility, which always required a personal guarantee.

That's why I was always responding to box numbers (the small ads) in the *Financial Times*, even as the company was doing well enough to expand and take on an additional negotiator and a full-time book keeper. After I responded to one advert offering finance for property schemes, I got a phone call from a financier called Pat Matthews, who was managing director of Estates Property Investment Company (EPIC). He was closely connected with the Ionian Bank – owned by Michael Behrans and Tim Trusted, both former stockbrokers who'd made a fortune on the bond market. They had a strong appetite for property finance, having just successfully floated EPIC on the stock market.

I went to their offices at Park Place, Regents Park, to meet Mr Matthews and EPIC's chairman, Bert Perry. The meeting was a great success, leading to the formation of a joint-venture using a shell company I owned – appropriately named Factory Holdings Group Ltd – into which EPIC transferred a 25-acre industrial site at Catcliffe, near Sheffield. Though I could not have guessed it at the time, this was also the start of a long-running business association, for I would continue to work with Bert Perry on numerous projects over the next 45 years.

It looked like we were set for big things. EPIC's public relations company put out a press release about the tie up and the story ran in the national and property press. I then received something that gave me

PROPERTY FIRM PAYS £75 FOR £150,000

FACTORY HOLDINGS GROUP, a privately-owned firm which owns land in Leeds, Cardiff, and Sheffield valued at £200,000, is selling out a 75% interest ... for a mere £75.

Buyer is Estates Property Investment. But in return for getting the controlling stake, Estates Property Investment will pump an extra £1,000,000 into a project to develop the property sites.

The remaining 25% share interest in Factory Holdings will be shared among 57-year-old Armand Felix and 28-year-old Leslie Brown—joint founders of the firm.

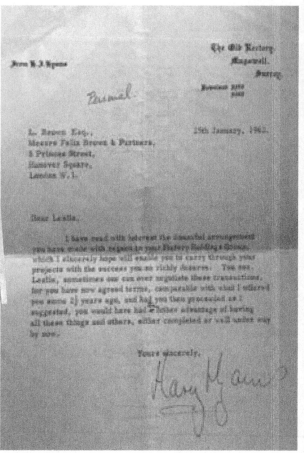

Above: EPIC deal reported in the *Daily Express*, January 1962
Left: Harry Hyams' letter to me after the deal was publicised

cause for concern – a letter from Harry Hyams, my former colleague at Hamptons. While wishing me every success with FHG he said that I should have accepted the similar offer of finance he'd made to me two years earlier. I remembered discussing finance in broad terms with him, but I honestly do not recall him making any firm offer. I would certainly have taken him up on it if I had realised he was serious... and to this day, not going with his offer of backing is one of the few things I regret in my entire business career.

Even so, things were going very well with the business. EPIC were as good as their word, funding developments in Glasgow, Wrexham and Bath. Demand for modern premises was high all over the country and we kept expanding. I was following the motorway expansions – anywhere there was a motorway or trunk road being built, I was searching for sites in the immediate area. Of course, Armand Felix was still involved in the company at this point. I could see he didn't have the necessary skills to assist in our rapid expansion – but he was still entitled to a third-share of the profits. This was a truly unfair position. I was scouring the country to find further sites, securing new tenants – and organising the finance required, when his original role in the business had been to provide the finance.

Above: Stover Trading Estate near Yate in Bristol
Below: Regent House, Wrexham

In the end I just spoke firmly to Armand. He was naturally hurt – because he felt he'd given me my initial opportunity – but I couldn't let the existing position carry on, as I could clearly see which way the business was moving. I had numerous developments in hand and more sites were being acquired, but sadly Armand was unable to contribute to this growth. This now had to come to an end. He was bitter, but I was adamant and eventually, in 1962, I acquired his holding and changed the name of the estate agency practice to Leslie L Brown & Co.

I took the view that large-scale development on a speculative basis was the only way forward and, at the time, few had the financial ability or nerve to entertain such an idea on a speculative basis.How would a council like Sittingbourne District Council hope to see a site of 46 acres developed? Nobody else was able to take on something that large in those days. But FHG would. We were the answer to the council's prayers, because we could commit to a big project – but they were also the answer to our prayers, because this site gave us the opportunity to put our development strategy into effect.

Sittingbourne was my first really big development with EPIC – and it came about because of a chance call to the town clerk's office saying, "We're looking for sites in the Maidstone or Sittingbourne area". The town clerk himself called back to say they knew of a site close to the town that had recently been zoned for industry. He made an appointment for us to meet the vendor, a farmer – and I still remember him driving us around the site in his battered old car, sliding on the mud. We agreed a deal to acquire the land and start the

A full-page story on the Trinity Trading Estate in the *East Kent Gazette*, April 1966

development, which we named the Trinity Trading Estate. It opened in 1964 and it's still there today, but it's grown bigger as the council has zoned more and more land.

We were developing sites all over the country: at Seacroft, near Leeds; in Southampton; in Rugby; at Yate, near Bristol; in Altrincham near Manchester; and in the Cheadle Hume district of Manchester. The Stanley Green scheme in Cheadle Hulme was one of the earliest, starting in 1964. It was a brave deal, let me say. There was a motorway designed

Development	Location	Area (acres)
Seacroft Industrial Estate	Leeds	8
Chandlers Ford Trading Estate	Southampton	10
Tribune Trading Estate	Rugby	14
Stover Trading Estate	Yate	20
Broad Heath Industrial Estate	Altrincham	20
Stanley Green Industrial Estate	Cheadle Hulme	42

Above: A half-page on Cheadle Hulme in *The Sunday Times* plus an aerial view of the Stanley Green Trading Estate, before the motorway was built

to rise over the site entrance. The whole site covered 42 acres, but it came in two adjoining parcels of land involving two separate owners. One half of the site had drainage, the other had electricity and access. So we bought them together – but then we had to create a master design, right down to working out where the estate roads were going to go and how it would all fit together.

Our overall approach was to start building work as soon as possible on each site, putting up a number of single-storey industrial/warehouse units, varying in size from 3000-25,000sq-ft. This first phase was always speculative to encourage demand. We employed several architectural practices who would design – subject to our approval – these buildings, to ensure we got planning consent before seeking tenders for the construction work. Inevitably, sometimes there were delays with planning approval, but we always received consent in the end.

Surprisingly, we found that it took months at most of the sites for local industry to realise exactly what was happening. The large scale of these projects was generally new to most of the locations where we were operating. Local and national agents would be invited to come and see

35

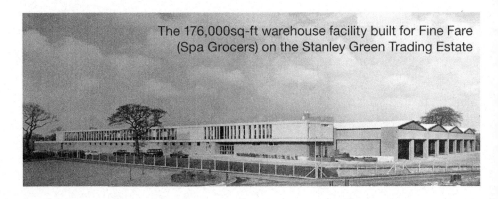

The 176,000sq-ft warehouse facility built for Fine Fare (Spa Grocers) on the Stanley Green Trading Estate

our developments first-hand – and soon we found that buildings were being let and reserved so fast in some locations that the second phases were needed urgently.

The Stanley Green Trading Estate in Cheadle Hulme was so successful that several buildings in phase one were let before completion. Developing the site took several years and as further phases were constructed, some buildings were designed to the tenants' requirements. These included a 176,000sq-ft distribution centre for Fine Fare – better known as Spa Grocers, a 50,000sq-ft rocket-research unit for Hawker Siddley Dynamics, a 25,000sq-ft office and research unit for Styrene Copolymers, a 50,000sq-ft distribution depot for Dimplex and, in 1969, a 55,000sq-ft headquarters-and-manufacturing unit for the large German firm BASF.

I cannot remember the name of the senior executive who came over from Germany – he had a formal German title of Von… and he made quite an impression on me. He was beautifully attired in a lovely tailored suit and tie. I met him on the site – he spoke perfect English – and here was a top industrialist coming to England to talk to me about the site we were developing. He was making sure, personally, that his company would get what they wanted. I understood that approach perfectly. I wouldn't let anything go forward until I was happy with it myself. I would never erect a building I did not approve myself.

As well as the bulk development of trading estates around the country, FHG also acquired many smaller, individual sites that were quickly and successfully developed. It wasn't long before FHG was one of the largest industrial-type property developers in the UK and further sites were constantly being offered to us. I'm not trying to make it sound easy, though. It wasn't easy. But frankly I was ahead of the game – miles ahead of it. Nobody else was doing what I was doing on such a scale and it was paying dividends.

Meanwhile, in 1968 or 69, EPIC had acquired shares in a company portfolio of investment property from a Leeds-based entrepreneur Fred Evans, whose son Michael was appointed to the board. Sadly, Bert Perry and the Evans could not see eye-to-eye on the direction of the company so, between themselves, decided to notionally split the company between Northern and Southern groups, to avoid open board-room warfare.

I continued to find and offer sites to EPIC but anything north of, say, Rugby became the Evans' domain – and this meant forming another, separate EPIC subsidiary, which was called Spabridge Investments Ltd. It quickly acquired two sites in Leeds: a 12-acre industrial site off the Dewesbury Road; and a site on Coburg Street in the heart of the city, bought from local architect J Stanley Wright. We built a 15-floor, 77,000sq-ft office building, Tower House, which was swiftly let to well-known companies. In all fairness, I have to say that father Fred and son

Started in 1969, the 55,000sq-ft headquarters for BASF was built to the firm's specifications

Tower House in Leeds, plus coverage in *Estates Gazette*, September 1968

Michael Evans did not interfere with these projects, board meetings were always professionally conducted and we became good friends.

However, for all the success we were enjoying, I could see a different and bigger future for myself, so decided to negotiate the sale of my shares in Factory Holdings Group to EPIC. During the negotiations, Bert Perry took me to one side and informed me in strict confidence that he was stepping down as chairman. He'd been gradually building up his own property business in parallel with EPIC and he was about to float it on the Stock Exchange. He suggested that, once our respective positions had settled down, we should get together and form a joint venture that his new company – Property Security Investment Trust Ltd – would completely fund in the same way that EPIC had funded FHG. But first, of course, I had to agree terms to sell my shares in FHG and set up my own group of companies.

Chapter Five
Consolidation

T he sale of my shares in Factory Holdings Group Ltd had given me a significant amount of money – but I wasn't looking to retire on it. Far from it. I was raring to start afresh, but this time I would do things differently. This time, I would ensure that my companies held on to all the investments we had built. That's how you get a strong position in the property business: by holding on. And the stronger your business, the greater its potential to grow. So it was essential to build up an investment company with a solid income base, preserving some capital for further in-house developments.

I set up a new company called Consolidated Factory Holdings Ltd which was incorporated in 1957. It's no coincidence that the name was so close to that of FHG. After all, I was setting out to continue with the same business model and it couldn't hurt if potential investors and property people were able to work out that the new company had some connection to the successful old one – which the name implied. I allocated minority shareholdings to the key members of my team: Bernard Tracey; company solicitor Jack Williams; and our talented quantity surveyor, Roy Kinsler.

The new business got off to a flying start with a warehouse development at Shannon Street in Leeds, pre-let on a long-term lease to Avon Rubber Co Ltd. This British tyre company was expanding rapidly and required additional outlets. Soon we had built premises for it in Bradford, Bristol and Gateshead – all let on long-term leases, and all secured with mortgages arranged through Jones Lang Wootton.

I'd been pleased with the speed and quality of the work on the Leeds site we'd developed for Avon, so I was more than ready to consider the contractors for other projects. Roy Kinsler, who as our QS worked closely with them, told me they were quite short of work so would be glad of any opportunity. "I think they might even fund it," he suggested. We put it to them and they agreed: if we negotiated future contracts exclusively with them, they would defer all interim payments during the construction period – leaving a single bullet-payment to be settled three months after the end of construction work. There's no way a contractor would work like that today – possibly they shouldn't have agreed to it then, but they did… and it was a great deal for us. It meant they would cover the cost of developing our sites and we wouldn't have to pay until the tenants were in and our long-term finances had been secured.

That negotiation came at the perfect time. I had just agreed terms to acquire a large site in central Middlesborough from the Constantine Shipping Company. It was zoned for offices and we were in the early stages of negotiating with Teesside County Council, which was looking for additional office space. Our architects in Leeds, the Hinde

Woodhouse Partnership, produced a set of drawings for a nine-storey, 50,000sq-ft office building with car parking. These were presented to the council and – subject to a few minor changes – met their requirements.

This would be a huge project, with two big potential risks for my new company: one would have been the cost of development, but our negotiations with the Leeds contractor had resolved that; the other

Teesside Council offices in Middlesborough

was that we hadn't actually legally acquired the site yet… I asked the chief executive of the council to give us a letter of intent, and to reserve the entire building – subject to agreeing construction specifications, lease and rental terms. He agreed to this, with a few conditions of his own to protect the council's interests. Everything fell into place: we made the land purchase and secured a 35-year lease to Teesside Borough Council; the contractors agreed to start work, funding the project themselves; and, to cap it all, Jones Lang Wootton negotiated a lucrative 35-year mortgage deal for us with the Prudential Assurance Company at a fixed 5½% interest rate, with no repayment of principle throughout the term.

Meanwhile, our good clients Avon Rubber Co were still expanding – and both they and rival tyre company Pirelli were looking for suitable depot premises to serve the Nottingham area. The problem was, we had already scoured the area and there was nothing available or remotely suitable. Eventually we found a potential site in a good location (Glaisdale Drive) that was available, owned by the local council. However, it would require extensive – and costly – excavation work to prepare it as the whole site was uneven, with steep contours.

We asked the Leeds contractors to check the site and advise us. Their engineers inspected it and got information from the council about the subsoil and available services. Their report was favourable, so we went ahead and acquired the land from the council. Our architects designed a terrace of four single-storey warehouse units. Pirelli immediately agreed to lease two and Avon one – and with three-quarters of the development let, it made it a highly profitable development. The last unit was taken by a solid local business, Thomas Cork Sales Ltd, which made display stands for Selfridges and other high-end stores.

This turned out to be a particularly profitable development for us and there would be no problem settling accounts with the Leeds contractor when their bill was presented, three months after their work on site was concluded. I remember sitting in a bar in Leeds with the chairman, shortly after the first tenants moved in but before his firm had submitted its invoice. Making polite conversation, I asked how the project had gone for them. "Well laddie," the chairman replied, sucking his teeth. "To be honest, we lost £15,000 on that job." I was taken aback slightly: this wasn't how the relationship was meant to work. I informed him that we would cover that deficit – which we could do while still maintaining a healthy profit. After that, there was nothing I could not ask them to do.

From this solid beginning, the company was moving forward at a healthy rate – mainly due to our national coverage, developing sites across the UK. We were getting direct enquiries from major manufacturing companies looking for local headquarters, distribution or service-centre outlets. Demand was so great we were also undertaking purely speculative development of smaller sites and these schemes were also generally quickly reserved and let in the construction stage.

By the second half of the 1960s, the business landscape was beginning to change. Large UK-based manufacturing companies were starting to merge, or acquire smaller competitors, and this activity generated a huge demand for more new buildings, all over the country. I saw that if we could offer these businesses a facility to create buildings to their requirements, on well-located sites in whichever region they required, our investment portfolio could expand rapidly and with virtually no risk. It was clearly the right idea at the right time and many of the national companies we approached responded favourably, presenting us with lists of locations where they required representation.

Of course, every opportunity comes with its own challenges and my small team was increasingly hard-pushed to keep up with demand. We were scouring the country for suitable sites, constantly meeting different councils and estate agents. The scale of absences from the office was noticeable in efficiency terms and I knew additional negotiators were needed PDQ.

By chance, a business acquaintance called Fritz Burnham contacted me to ask if I had an opening for a young man who was keen to get into the property business. We met, I outlined what was needed and he started working for us almost immediately: a big welcome to the business, Dick Freemantle. Shortly after that, he was joined by Bob Cox who had been working in the Industrial Agency of Chamberlain & Willows. Naturally, neither had any experience of development work, but they were keen and capable and shortly became invaluable members of the team. Dick Freemantle attended many business meetings with me and as a result we became good friends – and in later years shared a few holidays with our partners and we still meet occasionally for lunch, just to catch up.

Even as one problem was solved, it caused another. With Cox and Freemantle on board to ease our manpower issues, plus new secretaries and a senior book keeper to keep the back-office ticking over smoothly, our offices became overcrowded – we definitely needed larger premises. After a lengthy search, we located a suitable self-contained office building at 9 St George Street, off Hanover Square. I personally bought the freehold, though it required considerable internal renovation before it was ready for occupation so we didn't move in for nearly a year.

The bookkeeper was my wife Barbara's father, Jack Shine. A former racing bookmaker, he was a wonderful, kind man and he immediately made a difference to the office. When he started, we were having deliveries of stationary and other office supplies seemingly at random – they'd just turn up. Who ordered them? Nobody knew. Maybe nobody had... Jack got to grips with the situation, calling one supplier and telling them that if they weren't at our offices to collect the unwanted delivery in half an hour, it would be left on the street. After that, we received only the stationary we actually ordered.

Meanwhile, we were as busy as ever with developments, having purchased sites for major office projects in Reading and Sheffield. The 45,000sq-ft Yorkshire site went like a dream: while still being built, the ground floor was taken by Standard Chartered Bank, with Norwich Union Assurance agreeing to take the rest of the premises for their regional headquarters. Berkshire was more problematic, as new government restrictions had come into force, limiting office development. We decided to offer the land by tender, with offers invited for a 125-year lease. We accepted an unconditional offer of £115,000 per annum from a leading public property company: a sound and profitable transaction.

Chapter Six

A larger scale of development

As the company grew, so did the scale not only of our projects but also the obstacles we faced. A particular problem we encountered time and again in the mid-1960s was that government restrictions limited the size of manufacturing space to just 5000sq-ft per site outside specified development regions. This was curtailing and unfairly blocking development on some of our sites that were outside these designated development regions.

That wasn't the only problem we faced. The Board of Trade, a government department, was purchasing sites in development regions – the high-unemployment areas throughout North-East England, Wales and Scotland. It was erecting sizeable buildings on spec for sale or rent and effectively had a monopoly on all manufacturing requirements above 5000sq-ft, as industrialist and expanding companies looking for premises on that scale would usually start by contacting the Board of Trade... which would direct them to its own sites.

However, the Board of Trade did not control warehouse or distribution-centres developments, as this was outside its remit. It occurred to me that if we offered to finance and erect large-scale industrial buildings in the recognised development regions, we could anticipate a large ready-made demand for our development projects which would in turn save the government significant capital expenditure.

I wrote a carefully worded letter to the Board of Trade's main office in London, emphasizing the virtues of our proposal countrywide, assuming they would circulate it to the regional offices. I received just a single response from Mr Wood, the senior manager at their branch on the Team Valley Trading Estate, Gateshead. He raised a number of pertinent questions and suggested a meeting at their offices. During the meeting, Mr Wood asked if we had a limit on the size of project we would undertake. Not knowing where this line of questioning was leading, I simply said there was no upper limit.

He then opened up and said he was aware of a 132-acre site that had just been zoned for industrial use. Currently it was High Flatworth Farm at North Shields, Tynemouth. After the meeting I immediately went to inspect the site and was more than impressed with the location. It was level, had more than a third of a mile fronting onto a major new road that was being built – what is now the A19 dual carriageway – which led to the Tyne Tunnel itself (also still under construction at this time).

I contacted Mr Wood and told him we were willing to proceed, subject to terms and price. He put me in touch with the factor representing the vendor, who was the Duke of Northumberland. A week later a deal was agreed to purchase the site at £1925 per acre. A sizeable financial package and a long-term commitment was essential – and once again PSIT stepped in and offered me the financial backing not only to acquire the site but also, crucially, to plan an appropriate Phase One of development.

The first step was to research the North East and the local markets, working with all the Newcastle-upon-Tyne estate agents to assess the extent of enquiries in the area. I was very encouraged as there was clearly an unsatisfied demand across the board – particularly from companies seeking distribution and warehousing outlets. Even so, such a large development demanded extremely careful planning and the importance of road access to the site was critical to our final decision about what to erect.

We had appointed a talented young architect, Denis Lister & Associates, to advise

The design of the Tyne Tunnel Trading Estate was outstanding

A full page advert promoting the Tyne Tunnel Trading Estate (showing one of our buildings on the Tribune Trading Estate in Rugby)

us about the overall layout and he came up with a unique design for the buildings that produced an exciting appearance to the project. In the end, we finalised plans for a Phase One development that would see 50% of the main estate road installed, along with 26 buildings served by connecting spur roads. These buildings would be a mixture of sizes, from 3000sq-ft right up to 30,000sq-ft, with a total combined floor area of 265,000sq-ft.

It was a brave decision to erect so many buildings speculatively, but it gave us almost a monopoly on serious enquiries in the region and this quickly led to reservations and firm lettings on the premises under construction. The Tyne Tunnel Trading Estate became a very popular location and it wasn't long before all Phase One buildings were reserved. In addition, we were approached by Marks and Spencer, Twinings Tea Company and Spicers, agreeing terms to build large warehouse units to their requirements.

Big names like the Co-Op came to the Tyne Tunnel Trading Estate

A good range of unit sizes attracted a range of tenants to the Tyne Tunnel Trading Estate

We had submitted a sketch plan to another company for a large building fronting the new A19, with a firm rental quotation. The chairman was so keen to proceed that he actually called me while I was on holiday in Scotland, salmon fishing on the River Lochy near Fort William. He had already rung the office and was so insistent on speaking to me that my secretary Sonia Brahms had given him the phone number for my hotel. He range me there one evening and after a short discussion the lease and rent terms were verbally agreed.

The Tyne Tunnel Trading Estate was a great success – we built successive phases, working on it from 1965 until well into the 1970s. With this success and our other developments all performing well, we were experiencing serious, sustained and profitable growth. Our financial investor was always there and willing to entertain further projects. Which was encouraging, as the scale of the projects we embraced continued to grow. The next major project was to be the largest single building yet undertaken. Government departments occupied a number of

Some premises were built to the tenant's requirements

office buildings in the Liverpool suburb of Bootle – they were by far the largest employer of white-collar workers in North-West England. It was common knowledge that one of them, Giro Bank, was expanding and seeking more office space... but there was little available. We contacted Bootle Council about a well-located site it owned on Stanley Road, opening negotiations to construct a large office complex there. Naturally, we also spoke to Giro Bank about our proposed development and they expressed an interest – but they were unable to commit at the time without government authority.

Nevertheless, we continued our dialogue with the Bootle authorities and instructed Leeds architects Hinde Woodhouse Partnership to produce scheme drawings for a large individual office building with adequate car parking. They subsequently presented a unique and impressive design for a 20-storey 300,00sq-ft building of character, comprising 18 office floors over a two-storey podium designed to give importance and balance. At this point our quantity surveyors were brought in for a cost forecast – and they advised that as the floors were repetitive in design, construction would be relatively economic.

It was now up to us to decide whether to pull out or press on with the project, if we could find a financial backer. In view of the success of the Rugby, Haydock and Tyne Tunnel projects I arranged a meeting with Bert Perry, the chairman of PSIT. I gave him all the background details and left it with him to think over and let me know whether they would be willing to proceed or not.

At this time, I was in almost daily contact with PSIT about our other joint developments, but no mention was ever made of the Bootle project. I began to fear the worst and even began to look elsewhere for finance. Then one day, during one of our rare social chats over a cup of coffee, Bert Perry asked me what other projects I had going on outside our joint-venture company. I mentioned a pre-let we were tying up for the Avon Rubber Company on the Garrett's Green Industrial Estate in Birmingham. He then made me a serious offer: if we would agree to transfer this development into the joint company, PSIT would provide all the funds necessary for the very much larger Bootle office project. I didn't hesitate, of course.

Now I had the backing, the next step was to secure the land. We agreed a purchase price with the council, at the same time instructing the architects to advance their drawings to a level where we could obtain planning approval. It all went smoothly and we found Bootle Council incredibly supportive, as we were to learn later that they regarded our development as the focal point of the town's central area.

Tenders were invited for the construction and, on the advice of our consultants, the contract was awarded to Alfred McAlpine & Son as they had excellent engineers in-house who understood the complexities associated with multistorey buildings – back then, they were far less common than they are today.

We named the new building the Triad, on account of its shape. McAlpine moved onto the site in 1969 and before long the frame and floor structures were being cast and rising at an alarming rate. It was so comforting to see that we had such a knowledgeable and efficient contractor in place and

For many years The Triad was the tallest building on Merseyside

The Triad: a Bootle landmark and the northern home of the Inland Revenue

they'd erected the structure within 15 months.

The volume of this project was there for all to see and subsequently, as we had hoped, Giro Bank came forward to take space – though strangely they chose to lease eight floors in the middle of the tower, totalling 75,000sq-ft. It was good to have a tenant ready but their choice of floors was not ideal, as it split the tower into three sections. This affected the lettings of the rest of the building for some time, until the government itself came on the scene again as Giro Bank was downgraded and its operations split between other departments. It followed that various government departments then leased the entire 18 office floors in the building, with most of the accommodation occupied by the Inland Revenue – and I believe it is still in the Triad today.

Chapter Seven
High finance

Building any business depends on understanding the rules, especially the financial regulations – because sometimes they can work very much in the developer's favour. At a meeting with the company accountants, they mentioned that in view of our industrial development activities we were entitled to Industrial Buildings Allowance on premises let or sold to manufacturing concerns. Effectively 60% of the construction cost could be offset against profit tax in the first full year, with the balance over the following five years. This was of huge benefit to my business because the volume of new developments we were undertaking meant the accumulated IBAs represented a sizeable sum. Taxation on profits was never an issue for many years and, without having to settle a large tax bill, this gave us a greater ability to fund projects in-house.

Working in property development at any level inevitably means understanding how finance works, given the sums of money involved. The Ionian Bank had been a reasonable source of funding for many of my early projects and that continued even after I had begun working with EPIC. The Ionian's directors Michael Behrens, Michael Gaze and Stanley Fenn frequently invited me to lunch in their fine dining room at 64 Coleman Street in the City. These lunches, attended by many well-known business people, were always convivial as Michael Behrens was a wine buff and guests were all treated to an exquisite choice of premier and grand cru wines.

Over one particular lunch in 1971, questions were raised on a number of current business issues and I noticed that the bank seemed particularly interested in my own company's industrial-property transactions. Subsequently, I was invited to attend a meeting with the chairman of the bank and some of his colleagues, during which he said that as my company was a significant borrower of funds from the bank, the court of directors felt it appropriate to offer me a non-executive directorship. Naturally, I was taken aback but I accepted the post on the court of directors, which carried with it an acceptable remuneration package of £20,000 a year.

I was still working with the Church Commissioners as well. Their own normal long-term property investment was principally focused on farm land, central office buildings and shopping centres, but that didn't stop me approaching them with a development opportunity in the Surrey town of Byfleet, where we had just obtained planning approval for a 67,000sq-ft warehouse.

To my surprise the Commissioners agreed to fund the project on a 50/50 basis. While the building was still under construction, we let it to the Forestal Land Railway/Timber Company, which had large assets in South America. Shortly after, our tenant was taken over by Slater Walker Merchant Bank Group, so our investment became double secured. We eventually gained control of this building by acquiring the Commissioners' interest.

The direct-letting approach was certainly paying dividends and our development activities were spreading further afield. Sites were acquired and developed in Edinburgh, Glasgow, Carlisle, Lancaster, Preston, Durham, Teesside, Bootle, Liverpool, Manchester, Stoke on Trent and Derby. At our busiest period, we had more than 250 projects underway at the same time. They were all at different stages and some of the larger projects would last years – but that is just how active we had become.

All these developments demanded a large amount of in-house finance plus additional bank borrowing – but even that had its limits. If we were to continue our rate of expansion it would become vital to link-up with like-minded investors who would support us with a substantial line of funds. My first approach was to Bert Perry at PSIT, as the company had recently been floated on the Stock Exchange. I outlined our current projects and he agreed to form a joint company to develop future site-acquisitions, with PSIT providing all the finances required through Crusabridge Investment Limited.

It was not long before we made our first purchase for CrusaBridge: a 12-acre industrial site in Rugby, with extensive frontage to the Leicester Road, which we named the Tribune Trading Estate. We opened this project with a terrace of four smaller units and gave instructions to a local agent, who let all of the new buildings within a few months. In addition, we were approached by Khune & Nagel who required a new area headquarters office with warehousing. We built it – and a similar-sized building on spec that was let to the English Electric Company. There followed a firm enquiry from Berry Magicol and we built them a 60,000sq-ft distribution depot with offices. It was a wonderful start for Crusabridge Investments.

We were in regular touch with local agents across the country. In Cheshire, Lancashire and Yorkshire, we had apparently earned a reputation as a no-nonsense developer who performed to their word. As a

An early success for Crusabridge Investments: the English Electric Company's premises on the Tribune Trading Estate in Rugby

result, we were offered a 25-acre site at Altrincham, which we purchased using Crusabridge. While it was being developed, we named it the Broadheath Industrial Estate. Our partner seemed more than happy with the progress of Crusabridge Investments and was prepared to provide funds for many more site acquisitions.

It wasn't only agents who offered sites to us. I received a telephone call from a local building contractor who had a 42-acre industrial-zoned site fronting the A580 East Lancashire trunk road at Haydock in Lancashire. Was I interested? As luck would have it, one of my team was already in the area so quickly inspected the site and reported that it had great potential. I swiftly went north to view the land myself and arranged a meeting with the vendor, agreed a price and it became an important addition to our future-developments portfolio with Crusabridge.

Frank Smith at Warburgs contacted me and explained that one of the bank's important Swedish clients was urgently seeking several service-centre sites throught the UK, preferably on a rental basis. He told me I should get in touch with Peter Wallenberg, managing director of Atlas Copco, at their Hemel Hempstead HQ. I spoke to Mr Wallenberg and arranged a meeting at a London hotel. He was an impressive middle-aged

Haydock Industrial Estate: the development was kick-started by Atlas Copco

man – dynamic and clearly very intelligent. He described himself as a company doctor and he'd come to the UK after turning around his firm's South African operation. He would eventually become chairman of the parent company in Sweden but at this point he was here to resolve the problems of the British arm of the company.

Mr Wallenberg gave me a good brief on their space requirements and preferred locations. The Haydock site met their requirements in every way and, when I described it, he expressed serious interest – but wanted to see the site himself. Two days later he picked me up from London's Baker Street station at the ungodly hour of 4am, driving us up to Haydock in his Jaguar. We met our architects at the site and a set of lay-out drawings were produced and approved. Agreeing lease and rental terms was a hard-fought affair, but we eventually reached an agreement. This building kick-started development of the Haydock Industrial Estate.

While business was proceeding well, that could not be said of my personal life. I had met my second wife Barbara while we were both working at Leighton Goldhill – she had been a secretary there while I was a negotiator. We had two sons, Laurence and Michael, but I had felt there was something missing between us – even though we enjoyed the benefits of my business becoming more and more successful. We began to drift apart – and possibly the amount of time I spent travelling for business was partly to blame – but I was very generous and took pains to see Barbara shared in my success. She had couture clothing, mink coats, expensive jewellery, holidays and everything that went with our new lifestyle.

However, things came to a head after ten years when I discovered she was having a liaison with a Greek chap she had met on one of her many excursions to London. As far as I was concerned, the marriage was over. I moved out of the house, staying with my parents at first, and instigated divorce proceedings. My solicitor, who understood my personal and business circumstances, recommended a complete severance, so my wife would have no future come-back for additional payments.

I agreed to give Barbara our house in St John's Wood, all its contents, plus a sizeable capital settlement – even though she had announced she intended to set up home in Greece. Sadly, with my business commitments, I could not take on the responsibility for the children, so we agreed they would live with their mother and I would pay their school fees, though they would return to England in the holidays to be with me. The divorce was finalised in 1972. You may remember that I had employed my father-in-law, Jack Shine, as the office manager and bookkeeper, but the divorce did not seem to affect our relationship – he was a wonderful man and didn't let the change in our personal lives affect the work he did for me (and I suspect that secretly he rather took my side, rather than his daughter's).

However, leaving the family home and staying with my parents could only be a stop-gap after the marriage ended and I needed somewhere to live. I asked Dick Freemantle's secretary Jules, an upmarket girl, to help me find a suitable flat in the West End. It wasn't long before she suggested I inspect one in a new block just off Berkeley Square. It was spacious, came with parking, and was just three minutes' walk from the office – and it was equally close to Mark Birley's club Annabelle's, of which I was a member. I instructed my solicitors to pull out all the stops and the contract was signed within three to four days.

McKenzie, my interior designer, had completed the refurbishment of our offices and I met him at the flat, explaining the predicament I faced. He produced for me in double-quick time an outstanding home, furnished to my exact requirements and I moved in within three to four months. Once settled there, I enjoyed an active social life and at home I was admirably looked after by Miss Littleton, who would have a wonderful dinner ready for me at seven o'clock most evenings, or help out when I had guests.

Chapter Eight
Bigger and better things

I n the early 1970s the estates officer for the Sheffield Corporation
was a man called David George – a regular visitor to London,
promoting the advantages and development potential of his city. I
already had one site there on Church Street, waiting for the sitting
tenants to vacate so we could redevelop. So Sheffield was already on my
radar when Mr George came to see me. He explained the city council
was keen to expand Sheffield's central business area and had ear-marked
a sizeable site in Tenter Street for office purposes.

It certainly sounded appealing, as we had already seen with The Triad
how a supportive council could make a big difference to a large-scale
development. I went to Sheffield to inspect the site myself and while I
could see it had potential, it was also clear that piecemeal development of
such a large plot wouldn't be viable because of the overall accessibility
and the contours of the site – there was a significant change in height
from one side of the plot to the other.

We asked architects Oscar Garry & Partners to prepare a draft
development scheme. They came forward with a set of drawings showing
an imaginative development of five office buildings, with six levels of
underground car parking, providing a staggering 400,000sq-ft of space.
The design was totally flexible, taking account of the elevation changes
in the site, with floors on adjoining blocks at the same level so buildings
could be linked, if desired. We had the development costed out and,
while it looked possible and had the potential to return a healthy profit,
undertaking any scheme this size would be risky – even in Central
London where demand and rents would have been higher.

I persevered, agreeing terms with the Sheffield Corporation to acquire
the site but stopped short of legally committing to the purchase. As with

all things, timing is important. It was at this point we were able to settle in full all our financial commitments to our friendly Leeds contractors who had worked with us on so many of our other developments. They were very happy with our arrangement so far and were open to further projects… so I went to see the chairman at his home to discuss Sheffield. Would they fund this development, as they had the others? Almost immediately, he agreed and it was left for our architects and quantity surveyor to contact his team.

Even now, I hesitated. I wasn't looking to bring in an additional financial backer for this project. I was intending to fund it entirely through my business, with the assistance of our contractor. However, I was struggling to make the final decision: we had a strong balance sheet, but could I commit the company to a £7 million project when Sheffield was not at that time regarded as an expanding office location?

As I wrestled with this decision, matters were slowly proceeding. We had gone as far as obtaining outline planning approval for the scheme. In theory, we were ready. I arranged a further meeting with David George to have a frank discussion about the dilemma I faced. He reassured me – quite forcibly – that Sheffield Council's estates department received a regular flow of serious enquiries for office space… enquiries that could not currently be satisfied. That was why the full council had made the land available and that was why our Tenter Street site was central to their plans for encouraging business growth in the city. This was exactly the positive response I needed to hear – and it convinced me to go full-steam ahead with the development.

Things were also moving forward in my personal life around this time, with the divorce now behind me. I was friendly with Barry Dalton, whose family was famous for providing peanuts to most sporting and entertainment venues. His lovely wife Valerie invited me to a dinner party at their Hampstead home where I knew most of the couples, but to even up the numbers Valerie had also invited Linda Taylor (nee Chandler), who was recently divorced as well. Linda and I hit it off straight away and thereafter would meet regularly for lunch or to go to the cinema. Her family owned the renowned Walthamstow Dog Racing Stadium and she would take me there, where you could have a decent meal while watching the racing.

In Sheffield, our contractors moved onto the site in 1973 and began erecting the cranes necessary for the multistorey construction. In the hope of getting pre-lettings, we appointed Eden, Lockwood & Riddle as local letting agents and Jones Lang Woottan to cover London and the south. A development of this size and importance to Sheffield needed a distinctive name, so we named it the Pennine Centre. It was made up of five separate buildings: the largest was 13-floor Loxley House; the smallest was seven-floor Don House; Rivelin House and Shire Brook House both had eight floors; the development was completed by 10-floor Sheaf House. Between them they offered more than 250,000sq-ft of office space – on top of which the six-level underground car park had space for 483 cars.

I remember distinctly that, while the Pennine Centre was being built, I was inspecting a site in Exeter and had to call the office. I found a phone box – this was before mobile phones – and my secretary Sonia Brahms told me

Building	Floors	Area (sq-ft)
Loxley House	13	113,981
Rivelin House	8	40,108
Shire Brook House	8	40,076
Sheaf House	10	34,839
Don House	7	21,516
Total		**250,520**

Michael Newton of Eden, Lockwood & Riddle had called several times and needed to speak to me urgently. I called him and he told me, very excitedly, that he had been showing representatives of the Midland Bank around the Pennine Centre and they wished to reserve Loxley House, the largest of the five buildings. This was great news.

When I returned to London, I had several further discussions with Michael as the bank required more and more information, including architects drawings, to obtain board approval. Construction was fairly well advanced by this stage, but it did not seem to bother the bank unduly. They decided on several internal alterations, which they would pay for, requiring our contractors to undertake the work before the bank moved in. A full agreement on lease and rental terms was left outstanding, but the basic heads of terms was soon established so the bank could push forwards and secure board approval.

Unbeknown to our agents, though, Midland Bank had decided to transfer other departments to Sheffield. As a result, it would need more space... They decided to lease Rivelin House as well, as this was adjacent to Loxley House and the two buildings could be easily linked.

To demonstrate how goodwill can quickly get good results, our solicitors submitted a draft lease to the bank and about a week later their solicitors suggested we all went to Sheffield to see the development, so they could see the development first-hand and appreciate the layout properly. We met at St Pancras station, had breakfast on the train and the

The Pennine Centre stood out as a beacon in Sheffield city centre

two solicitors and myself huddled together – reaching agreement on all the terms of the lease before we alighted in Sheffield.

With the pre-lets to the bank in place, we instructed the contractor to concentrate on completing those buildings, including the bank's agreed specific fit-out, so they could move in and rental payments could come on stream. Among other things, the Midland Bank had specified external floodlighting, which made the buildings a beacon in the central area – and this alone highlighted the importance of the Pennine Centre to everyone who saw it. Midland Bank then took a third building and requested a name change that embraced all three, calling the linked offices Griffin House – reflecting the bank's corporate logo.

The two remaining buildings in the Pennine Centre were let to Manpower, a new government-sponsored organisation. Even with tenants in place, the long-term finance for the development required a lot of thought. Eventually, we decided it was most sensible to sell the investment and take the capital profit. Robin Broadhurst at Jones Lang Wootton introduced Legal & General Assurance and we finalised a deal to sell the entire project to them.

Chapter Nine

Europe – and home

At this point in my career, I had not experienced any major setbacks. I had tapped into the changes in British industry and had experienced some luck with the timings and the people I had met. My developments had been in popular demand. However, I was to have two that proved I was not infallible.

I was approached by Tommy Pike – my old boss at Felix & Partners, before I bought him out – who agreed to finance and develop a 10-acre site on an industrial estate in Cheltenham through a joint-venture with his firm Omnia Holdings Ltd. We erected six buildings, totalling 40,000sq-ft of space, anticipating an immediate flood of enquiries... but there was nothing. Even 18 months after construction was completed, we had received very few serious enquiries. It was an embarrassing and humbling experience for me. In the end, I transferred our entire holding to our partner without charge as a means of saving face.

I learnt another lesson about avoiding developing sites in fringe locations with a limited workforce nearby with an unsuccessful development in Scotland. We acquired a 10-acre site on the Whitehill Industrial Estate at Bathgate, between Edinburgh and Glasgow. This was in one of the Scottish Development Agency's specified development regions, so we erected two buildings each of 54,000sq-ft in the belief that we would place them quickly. In fact, enquiries were slow to come in and by the time we had let both buildings to the British Tyre & Rubber Company – on short, 10-year leases – we had made a financial loss.

Despite these setbacks, the business was experiencing sustained overall growth – not only through additional lettings on our trading estates but also through acquiring and developing several smaller sites. This success ensured we could absorb the disappointments of

Cheltenham and Bathgate. We were even able to start thinking about further expansion beyond the UK borders.

As ever, opportunities can come from casual conversations with the right person at the right time. Chatting with Fritz Burham, who was a small-time property-oriented person I'd known for some time, I mentioned we were thinking of developing on the Continent. He was keen to help out and quickly found us a potential site in Karlsfeld, a suburb of the Bavarian capital Munich, in southern Germany.

I'd never been to Germany before – my European travel had just been for holidays to Italy or the South of France – but it turned out that, unbeknownst to me, my senior negotiator Dick Freemantle spoke fluent German. The two of us went out to view the site and we made all the usual enquiries about demand, construction methods and general rental approach. The Karlsfeld site was owned and being laid out by a local builder, installing roads and services, and it was ideal for our kind of development so we agreed to purchase a plot of 12 acres.

Mr Burnham introduced us to a firm of advocates in Munich, who handled the purchase. They in turn introduced us to a local architect, Francis Kuhn. We outlined our development ideas to the new team and received incredible support. We were bringing English property ideas and standards with us – which was fairly new to them. Most German industrialists purchased their properties, so for us to erect premises only for rent was unusual. Our German team understood what was needed and we left the architects to produce a draft development layout.

Returning to London, my first priority was to find a financial backer for the project. I approached PSIT again, who were enthusiastic – and more or less agreed to proceed straight away, subject to advice on currency exchange rates. For this they turned to Brown Shipley merchant bank, who were experts on foreign-exchange issues. Brown Shipley Bank had been involved in the floatation of PSIT and was itself a shareholder in the company, represented on the board by Peter Dunn.

Mr Dunn arranged a meeting for us with a German bank in Frankfurt. We were welcomed royally and the German bankers were very enthusiastic about our plans, agreeing to provide the majority of the funds. The Germans were very keen to do business with the British. We then went on to Munich, quickly arranging a meeting at the advocate's office to thrash out a deal with the owner. After several hours, everything was agreed and Peter Dunn signed the contract on behalf of PSIT. In due course we began construction of a large terrace of inter-communicating buildings – and before they were complete, the entire development was let to a large local supermarket group.

Eventually, this investment was sold on doubly advantageous terms. Not only was there the normal developer's profit but also the exchange rate had moved substantially in our favour: bank finance for the project had been finalised at 10.2 marks to the pound, but when we sold the exchange rate was 4.5 marks to the pound.

Away from the office, my relationship with Linda had continued and while my team was working on the construction of the Pennine Centre we decided we should live together, so started to search for a suitable home. Linda viewed a number of possible houses in the London suburbs, but nothing appealed. Then one day a set of particulars for a house in Chalfont St Giles arrived in my office – which in itself was unusual. The

Farlands: an impressive and wonderful home. I do regret having sold it

house was to be offered for sale by auction and the particulars looked appealing, but neither Linda nor I knew anything about that area of Buckinghamshire. We decided to investigate the following weekend.

Linda and I drove around the Chalfonts and were impressed. Turning into Nightingale Lane, everything looked positive. There was the house, Farlands, with an agent's board outside announcing the auction date just five days hence. I drove down the drive and knocked on the door, without an appointment, but the housekeeper who opened the door showed us around anyway. We were now more than impressed – Farlands had seven large bedrooms and stood on a 10.5-acre plot with two self-contained modern cottages for staff. Nightingale Lane was clearly the premier address in the Chalfonts, as the neighbouring houses were of an equal scale and all of individual design.

With the auction looming, time was of the essence to arrange finance. As it happened, I was rushed off my feet in the office and didn't have time to organise the financial facilities. Nevertheless, Linda and I attended the auction in Gerrard's Cross and I secured the property with a bid of £168,000 – which was a sizeable sum in 1972.

Flushed with success, we rushed back to the West End to celebrate and, to commemorate the occasion, I decided to buy a ring for Linda. I parked my Rolls Royce outside Asprey's store on Bond Street but, to my embarrassment, I didn't have any loose change for the parking meter and had to ask Linda for a loan. I don't think she was too worried, as she was the beneficiary that day

While Farlands was being rennovated, Linda, the children and I lived in one of the cottages

of an expensive ring and a very fine house.

Of course, I had not actually arranged the finance for the house purchase… But Peter Dunn of Brown Shipley came up trumps and the acquisition proceeded smoothly. While

We had stables built to house Sarah's ponies

Farlands was a substantial property, it did need a great deal of updating so I again appointed TD Mackenzie, the interior designer who had refurbished both my offices and my flat off Berkeley Square, to give me a home of distinction. This was a major project, with fireplaces and chimneys to be removed and internal walls moved to improve the layout and give each bedroom an en-suite bathroom.

Outside, we had a swimming pool and changing rooms built, as well as a stable block for Linda's daughter Sarah to keep her ponies. While all this work was going on I moved into one of the cottages with Linda and the children. The works were not quick, so we were there for some time – but we functioned as an efficient family and it was good to be establishing ourselves in the Chalfonts, even if it felt at times as if the cottage was approached through a major construction site.

Once we were settled in Farlands, Linda's parents gently suggested it was about time we made our relationship official and in February 1974 we were married. We are still together so it really was a case of third-time lucky for me.

Chapter Ten

Hanover St George

After Germany, my next developments were closer to home. There was strong demand for warehouse space in close proximity to the City and West End. Peter Dunn of Brown Shipley rang me out of the blue to say that, if I needed assistance for any future projects, the bank would be willing to provide financial backing on a joint basis. This was a timely offer as the City of London Corporation had just accepted my bid for a site at Brewery Road near King's Cross Station.

Our architects had designed a terrace of four single-storey warehouses, which included first-floor offices. For this type of building, it was a sizeable development for central London, covering 34,000sq-ft. The bank agreed to finance it and we formed a joint company.

Over the next few years we acquired a further five sites in Brewery Road from the Corporation of London, constructing 18 commercial buildings that provided 275,000sq-ft of new accommodation. The largest

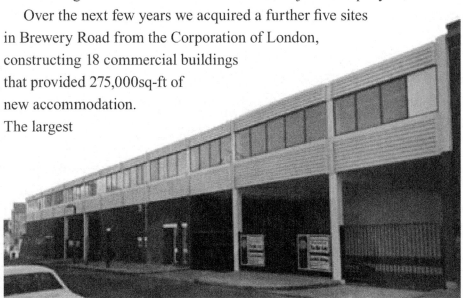

We developed six sites in central London, on Brewery Lane near Kings Cross

building was a two-storey, 97,750sq-ft property designed for and pre-let to the Chrysler Motor Company, for use as a central service/parts depot. Oddly, Chrysler required us to sign a confidentiality

Farlands' swimming pool and changing rooms

undertaking not to disclose their involvement with the building until the construction and fit-out was completed.

Away from the office, our family was settling into life in Farlands. Sarah and Butch, Linda's children, were attending excellent schools in Gerrard's Cross and as a result we met a number of families our age and had an active social life. With the building work finished, we moved into the main house (though the children missed the cottage) and entertained extensively – not only our new local friends but also many of my business associates.

In the summer months, the swimming pool was a boon for the children and their friends – though I have to say it was equally enjoyed by us adults. The foresight in having the changing facilites built for it really paid dividends now. As my divorce from Barbara allowed unlimited contact with my sons Laurence and Michael, at least half of their summer holidays was spent with us at Farlands or in Europe.

We were well established in the Chalfonts when, unexpectedly, my ex-wife called to talk about the boys. The headmaster of their school in Athens had expressed some concern about their behaviour and their academic progress. I immediately called the head, who understood the family circumstances, and he spoke very frankly: he thought it would be better for the boys if they returned to England and for me to take over their education PDQ. Following that disturbing conversation, I had an equally difficult one as I sensitively explained things to Barbara. While I was more than willing for this to happen and we had adequate space in Farlands for the boys, everything would depend on whether I could get them into a local school at short notice.

Linda went to see Maurice Avery, the headmaster at Thorpe House School in Gerrards Cross and explained our predicament. He did have space for both boys... but only if they were weekly boarders. We accepted this on the spot and I explained it to my ex-wife, who thankfully went along with the plan. Within a week Laurence and Michael arrived and settled in. The increase in our family kept us busy coping with all the childrens' activities – from Brownies, Cubs and Scouts to judo classes, cadet corps, football matches and gymkhanas.

It was now obvious that Linda needed help with the daily chores and upkeep demanded by such a large property with a busy family. Equally, I needed someone to take charge of the gardens, orchard and paddocks as this was certainly not my forte. After advertising in *The Lady* magazine, we recruited Arthur and Grace Skinner, who quickly moved into one of the cottages and rapidly proved their worth to us.

While we were in Farlands, my parents enjoyed their 60th wedding anniversary – a milestone that we marked with a large celebration. I wrote to Buckingham Palace, knowing that – like 100th birthdays – it was possible to have royal acknowledgment of such a rare anniversary. The palace wrote back to request copies of certificates, which I duly provided.

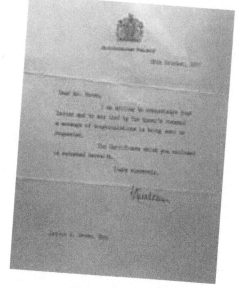

We prepared for a large party, with an extensive menu and wine list. I brought my brother Reggie and his wife over from Australia for the event. On the day, a representative of the Post Office – not a common-or-garden postman, but a gentleman in full ceremonial uniform – delivered a certificate from the Palace to commemorate the anniversary.

Business was still progressing apace throughout this period – with more notable developments in London. We acquired a 1¾ acre site on Wharf Road, off City Road near the Moorfields Eye Hospital, where we built a terrace of five warehouse buildings covering 78,500sq-ft – most of which we sold to the Prudential Assurance Company for long-term document storage.

There followed an extraordinary piece of luck, as the Corporation of London placed a further 1¾-acre site in North Road, off Caledonian Road, on the market. There was strong competition for this site from other developers, but given our successful developments in Brewery Road and our good track record, our tender offer was accepted. With backing from Brown Shipley Merchant Bank, we acquired the land and erected a terrace of seven buildings, with a floor area of 88,500sq-ft. Olympia Business Machines leased most of them and the remaining units let quickly.

We circulated a brochure introducing the new name of the company

The number of joint-venture developments we were involved with was now becoming an administrative nightmare – not least because each joint-venture company needed its own name and its own stationary. Knowing which to use was confusing for everyone, myself included. I discussed this problem with the office team and it was unanimously agreed that we should adopt a single corporate title.

Many corporate names were considered but, in the end, we chose Hanover St George Securities Limited, as it reflected the location of our offices and it was a sound name to promote. In view of our ever-closer relationship with Brown Shipley Bank, we allocated them a 5% shareholding interest and Peter Dunn accepted a position on the board. In the months that followed, we transferred all our direct property investments into the new parent company, as well as our holdings in all joint ventures. This created a single, sizeable, profitable enterprise.

Our first project, funded with in-house money, was the acquisition of a 10-acre site on the DragonVille Trading Estate in Durham. We built two self-contained industrial units with office space, each having a floor area of 53,000sq-ft. Mono Containers Ltd, already on the estate, agreed terms to lease one building and the other was taken by the Ministry of Works, to use as a training establishment to teach engineering, bricklaying, joinery and many other trades.

With our track record for developments, we were receiving a steady string of serious enquiries. Some came from our existing tenants, looking for additional outlets, but plenty were from new companies urgently seeking premises in locations across the country. Our development programme expanded dramatically to absorb this demand – we and our solicitors were kept busy tying up pre-letting agreements.

These were exciting times at HSGS and the company income rose substantially over a relatively short period. In view of the covenant strength of our tenants, we decided to retain most of the investments for long-term growth rather than, as I had done in the past, sell properties upon completion. This required a different form of finance so mortgage facilities were organised with Confederation Life Assurance and Sunlife Assurance of Canada.

Chapter Eleven
Selling up

The formation of Hanover St George Securities Ltd meant that it became easy for people outside the business to identify our success. We had always known how well we were doing – and perhaps some of our partners had understood that – but when your holdings are spread through a number of joint-venture companies, it takes an expert eye to see the bigger picture. Once we had brought our investments under the single HSGS banner, I began to get an increasing number of enquiries about mergers or selling the business.

The first one I took really seriously was an approach from Charles Knight, who had taken over as chairman of EPIC following the departure of Bert Perry. He made contact to discuss matters of mutual interest – after all, I was still a significant shareholder in several of EPIC's subsidiary companies. As Mr Knight was also a director of the Phoenix Assurance Company, EPIC's largest shareholder, he invited me to join him at the annual property-industry profession luncheon, which was held at the Savoy Hotel, hosted by Gerald Ronson of the Heron Group.

Mr Knight proposed a merger. His suggestion was that EPIC would immediately acquire HSGS at valuation, via a share exchange. I would be appointed chief executive of the enlarged group – with an undertaking from the board that I would be appointed chairman within two years.

This proposal had a great deal of merit for me personally, for as well as reuniting me with all the developments I had previously sold to EPIC, it would convert my shares in the private company into those of the larger and publicly listed one, where they could easily be sold on the stock market if I ever need to realise their value.

This wasn't a deal I could have considered if Bert Perry had still been at EPIC. As often and as profitably as he and I worked together on so many projects over the years, I don't believe I could have worked so closely with him. He was always supportive of my developments, but he was a very demanding man and could be difficult to work with at times. At least with our relationship, I could walk away when I needed to. I could not have done that if our companies had merged.

Charles Knight was a different character and after serious consideration, I told him I was prepared to proceed, subject to agreeing the valuation of our respective properties and my approval of the entire EPIC property portfolio. Jones Lang Wootton were instructed to prepare a valuation of the HSGS properties, while EPIC provided a detailed schedule of all its properties and we began to inspect and evaluate them.

It soon became clear to me that while the HSGS properties were relatively new and let on long institutional leases, the EPIC portfolio was not nearly so healthy. It was a mix of some good investments, some older let properties that could not be improved for several years… and a large disused airfield outside Cardiff with no planning approval. This coloured my attitude to the possible merger.

Still, I submitted the JLW valuation of our properties to Charles Knight. While I left him to review it, I agonized for some time about inheriting a portfolio of properties that, for the most part, did not compare with the properties I was about to pass over. In the end, I decided not to proceed with the merger – which seriously upset Mr Knight, as he had not expected that outcome. Though to be honest, neither had I. To sweeten the break, I paid all the costs of the abortive deal that he had incurred.

While this disappointment was unfolding behind board-room doors, the HSGS front office was as busy as ever. Our developments continued at an impressive rate and it became clear that the size and volume of developments was beginning to outstrip our internal financial resource. We could still continue to expand by seeking additional joint-venture partnerships, but I took the view that this approach led to us giving away far too much equity in our developments. To try to find a way around this problem, I arranged a meeting with Peter Dunn at Brown Shipley Bank's smart new offices in Founders Court to discuss our options.

Everything about the future pointed to a public flotation of Hanover St George Securities on the London Stock Exchange. Brown Shipley prepared a very detailed prospectus about the company, outlining the firm's history and the directors' backgrounds, illustrated by a selection of photographs of some of our buildings. It was a very professional document that was then distributed to other banks, institutional lenders and financial bodies, with the aim of securing tranches of finance before the actual stock market flotation.

Unfortunately, the timing could not have been worse. It was the early 1980s and the UK was experiencing the first bite of a serious financial crisis that, as it deepened, would restrict corporate borrowing across all sectors. The lack of confidence and capital in the market put a significant dent in our flotation plans. Brown Shipley Bank had already agreed to provide £2 million, but the only other interested party was the financial division of the American Greyhound Bus Company, which gave us a further £2.5 million facility – but that was all. This was a far cry from what we had anticipated so we aborted the flotation.

The location of HSGS developments at the time of the proposed flotation

Raising far less money than we had expected seriously affected our strategy over the two or three years that followed. Bizarrely, work on developing industrial warehouse buildings continued more or less as normal and we were still letting premises across the country, but at a noticeably reduced rate. However, the banking crisis meant it was a very tough market. There was much less finance available – and at borrowing rates of 13-15% per annum. Even long-term commercial mortgages were at this level and it was obvious that the property industry could not function properly or profitably with these interest levels. Property values were affected and even national house builders were caught up in the capital shortage, cutting back their building programmes. It was a desperate period for everyone.

Thankfully, by the mid-1980s we began to see the market recover. Indeed, it was fairly vibrant with enquiries for industrial and warehouse space on a sufficiently large scale to encourage some speculative development again on the land we already owned and on some of the trading estates. These confirmed the improvement in the market, many new lettings were concluded.

Unexpectedly, around this time we also became involved with office development in the London suburbs. It came about as a direct result of Bernard Tracey's friendship with a senior manager at the British Rail Property Board, who were marketing surplus land adjacent to suburban stations for office developments. Over a period of three years we acquired sites adjoining the stations at Tolworth; at Norbiton, near Kingston-upon-Thames; and at Cheam in Surrey. We created a total of 51,000sq-ft of office space with these developments, letting them to well-known companies.

We were getting solid coverage in the press for our development activities – not only in the *Estates Times* and the *Estates Gazette* (the bible for banks, institutions and everyone connected with the property profession) but also in the *Financial Times*, particularly in the Friday property column by Michael o'Hallowen and other journalists. This elevated profile meant I received several unsolicited approaches from property companies interested in mergers or even in taking us over completely – all of which I ignored as being premature.

I can't say I did not think about it, though. I had built the business up once, then pulled back from my close, early association with EPIC because it had involved giving away too much equity, only to build the property empire up again. Hanover St George Securities had weathered the banking crisis and was once again flourishing... but what did I really have to show for it? I was still working extremely hard, but my worth was mostly tied up in the company. Though none of the proposals I received was half as appealing as the EPIC merger suggested by Charles Knight, you can only have so many approaches before you start to seriously think about whether you should be looking to entertain a sale.

At this time, of course, HSGS was doing well. We were working closely with the conglomerate Thorn EMI Electrical Industries, which was always expanding and we had many of its subsidiaries occupying our buildings. We were in constant touch with Ken Wakeling, the estate manager there. He let us know that the trustees of the Thorn EMI pension fund were keen to invest their substantial funds in property... but competition was fierce and they were frequently being outbid.

Then one day Mr Wakeling invited Bernard Tracey and me to a lunch meeting, in the course of which he suggested that the pension fund could be interested in buying the entire shareholding of HSGS – at a full valuation of the underlying property portfolio, plus an allowance to cover the significant tax benefits of the company's sizeable Industrial Buildings Allowances. He made it clear that any deal would include only the let properties producing an income and that any sites held for future developments would have to be excluded, transferred out to a separate holding company.

At this point, I had perhaps convinced myself that I was ready to sell when the right approach came along. This sounded like it might be an offer worth considering, so we left Mr Wakeling to consult the pension trustees, obtain their approval in principle and confirm their full conditional offer in writing. Meanwhile, I went to see Peter Dunn at Brown Shipley, to find out what he thought of the deal.

As well as being very senior at Brown Shipley, Peter Dunn was a director of HSGS, representing the bank's 5% interest in the firm. He thought the overall proposition had merit – as the share-sale proceeds would settle any debts attached to the retained sites, putting us in a far stronger position to be able to develop them. Importantly, the deal with Thorn EMI would not need approval from the mortgage-holders of the HSGS let properties, because even though we would be selling the controlling share in the company, this would not affect the underlying property assets on which the mortgages were secured.

Perhaps unsurprisingly, the Thorn EMI pension fund trustees gave their blessing to the scheme, so both sides instructed solicitors. Given the size of the transaction and the large number of properties involved, it turned out to be a long process as many legal and technical issues had to be satisfied... not the least of which was what the net purchase price of the shares would be. After several months, the wording of the contract was finalised to both sides' satisfaction and our accountants were able to report what the pension fund was going to pay for our shares.

Everything was prepared – share-transfer forms were drawn up and a completion date was agreed – but unbeknown to us, Thorn EMI had instructed its PR department to announce its acquisition within minutes of completion. The sale went through in May 1977 and was highlighted in the London evening papers that night, as well as making headlines in the daily press next morning and in all the property journals.

Chapter Twelve

Forneth

With the bulk of the HSGS portfolio gone, I began to concentrate on developing or disposing of the remaining sites – the unlet properties or land that had been excluded from the sale and transferred instead to another company that I controlled.

One of the assets we'd been left with was an ultra-modern 107,000sq-ft industrial property in Leighton Buzzard, acquired from Golden Limited (better known perhaps as L'Oreal of Paris). We began offering the premises and almost immediately received a firm rental offer from the Rank Xerox Corporation. However, before terms could be finalised, Unilever inspected the site and made a firm proposal to buy the freehold on behalf of its Lipton Tea Company subsidiary. That was an offer too good to refuse.

Another site we owned was on the A5 at Bletchley. It had received planning permission, so I negotiated a contract with our loyal Leeds-based contractor and they began work on an ambitious 105,000sq-ft single-storey warehouse. It was a bold scheme, but the site could not be faulted as it was on the edge of Milton Keynes, which was expanding rapidly. Even the Milton Keynes Development Corporation expressed an interest and began offering the development on our behalf.

Shortly before the building was completed, I took a telephone call from the property manager at TESCO, who said that he'd inspected the development and the supermarket would be interested in buying rather than leasing it. We started negotiations and, out of the blue, he asked if I had ever been an office junior in the Hamptons accounts department. I was flabbergasted – then he added that his wife, who I'd known then as Peggy Elliot, sent her regards… The property business really is a small world and though this association had no bearing on the outcome of the sale, it did ensure the process was very smooth with no messing about.

In Scotland, we had already enjoyed great success without our developments on the East Main Industrial estate at Broxburn, outside Edinburgh. A local agent there alerted me to the fact that the council was increasing the size of the estate. I didn't hesitate to express an interest and, given our development history on the site, the council offered us a prominent five-acre plot facing the main roundabout on the estate. Architects W Patton Orr & Partners, who had designed the earlier phases, produced a scheme for six terraced single-storey units on either side of a central road, totalling 64,000sq-ft. The building contract was awarded to our friends in Leeds and, in property terms, the project was an immediate success with four units let to Trustee Savings Bank, two to Brinks Matt, and another building let to Lorrileux & Bolton, a specialist ink manufacturer controlled by the French government.

However, our limited stock of sites was rapidly being developed and we faced stiff competition when trying to acquire replacements. This had a negative effect on office morale. We were geared to deal with multiple projects but the fact is we were nowhere near as busy as we had been in our heyday. I had hoped the sale of HSGS to Thorn EMI would see me acquire a selection of new sites and build up a third property empire, but the world had changed and it was not so easy as it had been.

Senior members of the team became restless. First Dick Freemantle left, with my blessing, to set up his own company. Shortly after, Bob Cox did the same. Sadly, Jack Shine – my former father-in-law, who had worked for so many years as office manager and bookkeeper – was diagnosed with cancer and passed away within weeks, with Bernard Tracey and me at his bedside in the Middlesex Hospital. He had been an invaluable part of the team, keeping things running smoothly and he would have been hard to replace.

While these departures were not entirely welcome, they were perhaps inevitable and they forced me to reassess my own future. I sat down with my co-director Bernard Tracey and suggested I buy him out at a generous rate – very timely for him, as he was struggling with an expensive divorce. While I was not going to stop my development activities, I did reduce them greatly – not least because I had finally realised a childhood dream and acquired my own country estate.

It was my time as an evacuee that planted the love of the countryside in me, especially those visits to Mrs Bristow's parents' farm. Since boyhood, I had dreamed of owning a farming estate – and I had frequently discussed it with Linda. The sale of Hanover St George Securities had given me the capital with which to make this dream a reality – and the scaling down of my development activities provided me with the time to devote to it.

First, of course, I had to find the right farming estate. From our travels around the country, Linda and I decided Northumberland was our favourite county. I spoke to Colin Steel-Strang, senior partner at Knight, Frank & Rutley's Edinburgh office and was duly sent details of various farms – none of which appealed. After a few months of fruitless searching, Colin rang and asked if I would be prepared to pay for a "wanted" advert in *The Scotsman*. I agreed...

Knight, Frank & Rutley received only one response to the advert, from the factor of the Forneth Estate, near Blairgowrie in Perthsire. This property could be acquired off the market, so Colin arranged an

inspection for us. We were interested... though Forneth House itself had an unusual layout, in that the owners had blocked off the upper floors, removed the staircases and lived entirely on the ground floor, bungalow-style.

That set the tone for the whole property, as

Forneth House: a magnificent structure

the farm was generally run down and large sections of the land had been let to various parties. The land was a mixture of arable, grazing for livestock and some really lovely, stately woods with sporting rights. The whole estate covered 1750 acres, with five let

When we first visited Forneth, only the ground floor was inhabited, with the rest sealed off

farms leaving about 1000 acres in hand. There were also 10 let cottages, forming the greater part of Forneth village.

It was a sizeable property, but in a poor, rundown state and the house was very large. I wasn't sure. Linda and I discussed it, deciding to go back for a second "take it or leave it" inspection. It was a lovely day and the setting, with the view from Forneth House overlooking undulating countryside and Cluny Loch, is for my money one of the finest in Scotland. Despite our reservations, we decided to make an offer. After a little to-and-fro, we acquired the whole estate on favourable terms.

To advise us on essential improvements to the farm, we appointed Geoff Scarr of Knight, Frank & Rutley as factor. Between us we devised a master plan that involved creating a large central cattle court, with hard-paved access roads and an extensive fencing programme. We also

The view over the Forneth Estate, including the farm and village.

The farm was extensively modernised, with all the land under direct control

proceeded to buy out the tenant farmers, taking every part of the estate in hand under direct control to improve the farming process.

We installed central heating in staff cottages and extended the farm-manager's residence as well as the east lodge residence at the entrance to the grounds of the main house. I also got in touch with the Game Conservancy, who sent an expert to advise on additional planting to improve the shoot. To improve the farming enterprise we created, with the factor's advice, quality livestock herds. It wasn't long before farm manager Donny Lang was receiving rosettes for our animals at the local livestock shows.

Meanwhile, we had MacKenzie – who had had worked on my offices,

The estate included 10 properties in Forneth village as well as the farms

my flat and on Farlands – taking Forneth House in hand. His team of interior designers came up with a scheme to solve the internal problems of the house. The main staircase was reinstated to the original design, then many of the rooms were altered and new en-suite bathrooms created. The result was an integrated and modern

The kitchen in Forneth was the same as the one in Highgrove House

layout suitable for the whole family, with a rather fine guest suite with panoramic views.

We made regular visits from Farlands to view progress as the work proceeded, staying in the nearby Kinloch House Hotel. This was a substantial Scottish house run at the time by the Jennings, a husband-and-wife team who lacked the capital for many essential and long-overdue improvements. The beds were comfortable, but the rooms had limited heating so we often found my family or my shooting guests were the only people staying and we'd have the run of the place. In the end, one of the better reception rooms with a large fireplace became to all intents and purposes our private sitting room. Before every visit, we'd call Mrs Jennings and ask her to get plenty of logs in and light the fire.

As Forneth was finally completed, we found a buyer for Farlands and settled in Scotland – though I still had offices in London, which I attended from Monday to Thursday every week for a year. This was not a happy time for me or Linda – and she deserved a medal for everything she put up with at this point, living largely on her own in Scotland. She was concerned about me spending too many nights in hotels and suggested I buy a flat in London, for when I was in the office or even when the family visited the city.

I found and purchased the perfect property – a new four-storey terraced house in De Vere Gardens, Kensington. With four smallish bedrooms, a decent reception room, a dining room and a modern kitchen it fitted in with the London lifestyle and had far better facilities than any hotel. Even so, it still meant lots of travel from Scotland, leaving Linda alone in Forneth.

Finally, I decided this could not go on and transferred out of London completely, setting up admin offices in Forneth House for the farm and the remaining development properties. Now I was living there full-time, we began to create a social life for ourselves – but unfortunately Linda never quite settled there.

My London pied-a-terre in De Vere Gardens, Kensington

It must be said, we were something of an enigma or a curiosity for many of the local people. We'd arrived and made many costly improvements to the house and farm, but where had we come from? I heard one rumour that I was somebody in the Aberdeen oil industry...

Still, the farm was beginning to pull together and the shoot was a great success. We increased the number of birds put down, so the bag each shoot day would be around 200 birds, with a good mix of partridge and pheasant. Shoot days were always such happy affairs for everyone – not only the guns, who enjoyed superb lunches in the house, but also the beaters. Guests began to invite me on their shoots and Peter Ord, the factor at the Glamis Estate, invited me to join Lord Strathmore's private shooting syndicate, which met at Glamis Castle.

The children were all well settled as boarders at Strathallen School and in winter months, Forneth House became a regular port of call for the school bus on its way back from the Glenshee ski slopes. We seemed to be running a Little Chef for them and their many school friends – and we enjoyed every minute of it.

We had only been living in Forneth House for a few months when strange things began to occur. It started on the second floor, when a glass chandelier shattered into a thousand pieces, followed by all the bulbs popping out from another chandelier. Another time, I was hanging a picture and became acutely aware of some sort of presence, watching me, which was very disconcerting. I mentioned it to Andy McKenzie, my gamekeeper, who laughed and said it was well known locally that part of Forneth House was haunted.

I put this all out of my mind for some time, until I happened to meet the local vicar. Suddenly it all came back and I told him about the strange experience with the chandeliers and my sense of a presence and being watched. He offered to help by exorcising the affected part of the house, but then added it would be much better for me to deal with it in my own way. I waited until everyone else was out, then went upstairs to the area in question and shouted, "Enough is enough." Then I pointed out that whoever it was should be delighted to live in such lovely, friendly surroundings. That was the end of a very odd saga and nothing untoward ever happened again.

I expanded my Scottish sporting interests when I was contacted by David Laird, a solicitor who had represented me when buying Forneth. He was also the factor in charge of Lord Mansfield's Scone Estate and had got word that Lord Stormont (Mansfield's son) was considering selling the famous Stanley Beat on the River Tay. Would I be interested?

As it happens I had fished Stanley a year or two earlier and caught many salmon, so I was interested. I asked for the formal record of catches over the past five years, which showed an average catch of 385 salmon a year – which was impressive. I made an offer and, after only a little haggling, found myself the proud owner of one of Scotland's most famous salmon-fishing beats.

My plan was to put aside one day a week for me to fish throughout the season, then let the other days out to defray the cost of having bought the beat. Instead, I was approached by Jim Slater – a successful banker – who had formed a company called Salar Properties Ltd. He was buying famous fishing beats on a grand scale, on all the recognised salmon rivers, with the intention of selling rods on a time-share basis. The offer he made me for the Stanley Beat was just too good to refuse and I turned a tidy profit on it. Slater's idea was a good one, though – and he made another fortune with his river time-share scheme.

As diverting as the shooting, fishing and farming were, I have to admit I didn't fully settle into the new life. I missed the buzz of activities London has always provided. Still, I knuckled down and tried to find suitable development opportunities in Scotland. I acquired a one-acre site in the nearby Almond Vale Industrial Estate in Perth, erecting a terrace of four units. I found another site in Glasgow for small service units. They were good sites, but it was still a struggle to find suitable tenants.

While I was trying to make a go of things, I could sense that Linda was seriously unhappy. She had no friends of her age living remotely near us and the house ran, if anything, too smoothly as we had two full-time daily help. She was lonely and bored and, when we rationally discussed it, we realised this was not likely to change. We were still a relatively young couple – but Forneth really needed an older family with at least some Scottish background.

On top of which, it was clear that property-development opportunities in Scotland could not match what could be achieved in England, but I had no intention of ever splitting my life between London and Scotland again. Linda and I decided we should sell Forneth and move back to England.

When we came to sell Forneth, Knight Frank & Rutley produced this superb brochure for the estate

Chapter Thirteen
Going to America

C ommercial conditions may have been tough in the UK in
the late 1970s and early 1980s, but I was always looking for
opportunities. When we were living in Farlands, Linda and I
became good friends with an American couple – John and Joan
Essenburg. When they decided to move back to the United States, John's
company gave him a position at a subsidiary based at Mount Pleasant,
near Charleston in South Carolina.

Once settled, the Essenburgs invited us out to visit them – and we
gratefully accepted their kind offer. In fact, we decided to make a real
holiday of it, spending a few days in New York first. While there we met
up with Charlotte Ford (of the motor-company Fords), who had been at
finishing school with Linda in Florence.

Charlotte had written a book – *Etiquette: Charlotte Ford's Guide to
Modern Manners* – and was booked to promote it on a radio phone-in show
in Washington, a few days after we met her. Incredibly, we had reserved a
car in Washington, to drive from there to Charleston. Hearing this,
Charlotte asked Linda to ring the radio station on a reserved line, giving her
a few questions to answer live on air – a great experience for Linda.

We stopped overnight on the way to Charleston in the historic town of
Williamsburg, but we found the journey far too long and boring with the
50mph speed limit on the interstate highways. By the time we reached
the Essenburg's new home, we were both thoroughly exhausted. Still,
they were wonderful hosts and made us very welcome, taking us to all
the prime tourist spots in Charleston: the Battery; the Straw Market; and
the shell of the World War Two aircraft carrier the USS *Yorktown*.

We had been enjoying the Essenburg's hospitality for a few days when
John mentioned that an upmarket holiday resort was being developed by

the Kuwait Investment Company at Kiawah Island, just a few miles outside Charleston. Given my background in property, he suggested I go and take a look at it – though perhaps he was just being kind, finding a way to give us a break from the four teenage Essenburg daughters who would argue incessantly over just about anything...

We booked ourselves into the Island Inn, which was the main focal point for Phase One of the development, duly attending a film show that spelled out the master plan for developing the entire island. It was a lovely site, with ten miles of uninterrupted sandy beaches. It was more than impressive and I confess that I was tempted to buy a plot there and then – but I managed to hold back, as it was still only the start of the development and it might still have ended up a disaster.

When we returned to Farlands, Linda and I reflected on what we had seen in South Carolina and decided we would take the family on holiday to Kiawah the following year. I spent the intervening months thinking quite seriously about the possibility of buying a plot there. Meanwhile, I had reserved a large seafront apartment for the family and, shortly before we left, my friend the art dealer David Mason contacted me: he said that if I liked what I saw and decided to invest, I should also buy the adjoining plot on his behalf. Stopping off in New York, I sent him a postcard with a picture of the twin towers of the World Trade Centre on the front. On the back I wrote: "Buying the one on the left. Do you want the one on the right?"

Linda and I go to inspect one of our properties on Kiawah Island

We took our connecting flight to Charleston and picked up our hire car from Avis, then drove to the island. I admit, I didn't know quite what to expect – but a transformation awaited us. The entrance to the Kiawah Resort was now gated, with security on duty to turn away those with no business on the island. Phase One was complete, with the Arnold Palmer golf course, tennis courts, a compact shopping mall and restaurants all open for business. The main estate road was about three miles long at this time and all the side roads giving access to the building plots had been finished. I thought the overall design was faultless, with every plot backing onto either a golf fairway or one of the manmade lagoons. In short, Kiawah was a tribute to what could be achieved in a very short space of time with a limitless supply of petro-dollars.

The children adored Kiawah and were very popular with the locals, who loved their English accents. Linda and I quickly decided that this was the ideal place for a holiday home, so we went to the sales office. After being shown what was available, we agreed to buy two plots on Phase Two in Surfsong Road – one for ourselves and one for David Mason. As I envisaged spending more time on Kiawah while our property was built, I also bought a lovely newly built condominium at 4555 Parkside, backing onto a large lagoon, so we would have our own place to stay while finalising the design and layout for Surfsong Road.

Design-wise, not all the homes on the island were to our liking but, driving around, we found one that did appeal which was nearly complete. I went in to have a closer look and was greeted by a young man called Brooks Fullerton – the architect! I explained why I was there and he gave me the guided tour. Then I took him to Surfsong Road, explained our requirements. He later came back to me with plans, which

Kiawah Island was my only foray into residential development

we amended, and finally a cost estimate, which we accepted – so construction commenced. Linda had already met with interior designer Patti Page and fitted out the Parkside property using samples and catalogues, so she was able to brief what we wanted for our new home. We returned to the UK

These were grand properties – but not so large as the mansions later built on Kiawah

knowing things would be ready in time for our next visit in the spring.

With my property hat on, I considered Kiawah to be ideal for some form of speculative house developments. I approached various men in the estate office sales team, as I suspected they had some prime plots up their sleeves – and I knew they'd like the idea of one fee on the sale of the plot and a bigger commission on the sale of a new house. Sure enough, several off-market plots were offered to me and I acquired a lovely site in Turnberry, two adjoining plots on Augusta National and a further couple of plots on Surfsong Road with views of the ocean.

Architect Brooks Fullerton produced an incredible set of ideas for individual developments on each plot and we began construction on two of the sites straight away. Things were going perfectly smoothly until Hurricane Hugo made landfall.

I was back in the UK at the time, but Linda was on Kiawah with the children. The island was in the path of the storm and I was worried. Neighbours advised Linda that the best thing to do was actually to stay put – the children even invited a few of their American friends over for a hurricane party while all hell was breaking loose outside.

The hurricane tore across the island, felling thousands of the mature trees and damaging properties. We were very lucky and our home and the development sites escaped largely unharmed. I was in regular touch with Linda and, once I was reassured the family was safe, my thoughts turned to the sale of the new houses. Naturally, I feared the worst – I imagined a hurricane would have a serious impact on demand – but I could not have been more wrong. Linda immediately sold both houses, getting the full asking price. On this basis, I told her she was wasted in the kitchen...

I still had three plots on Kiawah, with approval from the planning committee for houses, and I was determined these would be something special. Linda's mother had already been to visit and declared our house at 10 Surfsong Road to be fit for a film star, while Linda had been so taken with the project design at Augusta National she wanted to move in and keep that as our home on the island. We built and sold the last three properties very quickly, though the final costs were far higher than Brooks Fullerton's initial estimates so my profit was much lower than expected, but still worthwhile.

Sadly, Kiawah kept expanding and, for me, lost much of its charm as large tracts of land were developed, with mansion-sized houses that were hardly in keeping with the early designs. The main Kiawah Island Highway was extended a further five miles, more international-standard golf courses were built and the island has now become classed as a town in its own right. We sold up eventually and though we returned to visit friends, staying with Marg Middleton – one of the first residents – it wasn't the same place. Even Marg sold up in the end.

Chapter Fourteen

Twilight of a developer

When we returned to England from Scotland in 1984 I found that property requirements had changed. Shops in high streets were not so much in fashion and retail warehouses and retail parks were in vogue. I began to look for solo development sites on the edge of towns and it was clear there was no shortage of interest.

The company name I was operating under now was Blackfriars Securities Ltd. Jointly with Cromwell Holdings we purchased a site at Dartford in Kent that already had planning approval and initially agreed rental terms with Currys for a retail outlet. Our site adjoined a large retail unit owned by Texas Home Care, which was subsequently bought by Sainsbury's – who then approached us in the belief they could link both sites and put up a new supermarket. They offered triple what we had paid to secure the site, exchanging contracts within three days.

Supermarkets did appear to like taking charge of their own developments. Working with Cromwell Holdings again, I acquired by tender a siteadjoining Skegness railway station from British Rail. They had already secured planning approval for a 14,000sq-ft unrestricted retail warehouse. I began to offer the

We moved into Ivy House at Hadleigh Highstone, Barnet

proposed development to all the second-line food operators. Lidl made an offer to buy our interest in the site and leave the construction to them.

Meanwhile, I began developing in London again. My good friend Richard Denis-Smith at surveyors Jordan Salata had received instruction to sell a one-acre site in Acre Lane, Brixton. It had planning consent for an unrestricted retail warehouse of 12,000sq-ft. I met the chairman of the vendors, Marshalls Contractors, at their offices near Wandsworth Bridge and agreed terms. Detailed planning consent was obtained and we started building. Lidl again took a serious interest and, on completion, we sold the building to them for a substantial profit.

Richard Denis-Smith introduced me to another high-quality site in South London: a 1½-acre site at the junction of York Road and Lombard Road in Battersea, where Wandsworth Council had only recently given outline consent for non-food retail use, with the condition that half the site should be reserved for industrial use. The site was owned by Lonrho, who were keen for a quick sale and so had reduced the price accordingly.

I had again arranged finance for the project with Bert Perry's Cromwell Holdings – and he nearly lost it for us. He delayed and delayed until I was told that the deal was off. I called Mike Hastings, Bert's accountant, and told him we needed to move very quickly to retrieve some goodwill. He told me he was convinced he could get Bert's signature on the contracts, if I could get them to him. So I went to Lonhro head quarters in Cheapside – with no appointment – and announced my purpose at reception, asking to see the company secretary. To be honest, I didn't think I had a chance of seeing him, but after only a short wait I was actually shown in.

I explained that I was there to assure him the York Road sale could proceed and he paused before saying, slightly crossly, "Well you've messed us around long enough, you know." I apologised and promised that if we could get the contract now, I'd have it delivered to my chairman by motorbike and it would be back with Lonhro within 24 hours. The company secretary thought about this, then pointed a finger at me: "Alright, 24 hours. But that's it."

I stumbled out, amazed, and called Mike to tell him the good news – and the bad. The deal was still on, but we had to get the contract signed immediately. "Leave that with me," said Mike. We had the contract biked down to Bert in Poole in Dorset, he signed, and we got it back to Lonhro on time. The land was ours.

This wasn't the end of the drama with York Road, but the beginning. Our architects Martin Branston & Partners had drawn up an imaginative set of plans for a 14,000sq-ft retail warehouse with extensive car parking, plus a single-storey industrial unit of 17,500sq-ft. After consulting the planning officer, we made a formal application and it was approved by the planning committee. When we hadn't received the formal notice of approval after four weeks, I contacted the planning officer again. He revealed that the Labour Party members on the council had served formal notice on the chairman under local authority regulations, insisting the approval be rescinded on the grounds that the site should have been reserved for residential use.

As outline retail consent had already been granted before we became involved, I made an appointment to see the council officials and took my solicitors with me. It was agreed that our application would be considered by the full council… who were meeting about six weeks later. I went to the meeting and sat in the public gallery, watching proceedings and waiting for our case to have its turn. When it did, it was approved with no objections within minutes.

While all these problems were being resolved, our agents had been talking to several companies about the project. Staples the stationers made an acceptable offer for the retail unit and we sent them a draft lease for approval. Construction began but we were experiencing problems with the stationary company as it wanted more and more-expensive internal finishes included as part of the rental terms.

At this point, agents representing Halfords contacted me about the retail space. When I said it was already under offer, they emphasized that their client was very interested and would be prepared to offer an attractive rent to secure the property. Their property manager then called

Getting the York Road site developed was tricky but it was highly profitable

me direct, anxious to meet that day at any place that was convenient. As Linda and I had moved close to Barnet, I arranged to meet him for coffee that evening at South Mimms services on the M25.

When we met, I showed him the plans and answered all the usual questions about specification, before he finally put a direct question to me: what rental terms would I accept to change direction to Halfords? I quoted a rent £50,000 per annum higher than we had established with the stationers – and he agreed. We shook hands and an agreement for lease was completed within a fortnight.

The industrial unit on the York Road site was taken by a subsidiary of Perry Motors, but they were not ideal tenants as the use to which they would put the building was the repair of car-body parts, which is a messy trade. Eventually the company transferred elsewhere and the building was taken over by Big Yellow, who divided the premises into small self-contained storage units.

Chapter Fifteen

Bowing out gracefully

Though I didn't realise it at the time, York Road in Battersea was to be my final completed development. I did have one more project, in Brighton, but especially after the success of my earlier career, it was something of a damp squib.

I had found a site with good potential and negotiated terms, then again invited Bert Perry to get involved with the project. As with York Road, though, there was an interminable delay in getting a decision from him. It reached the point where I was convinced we would lose the site unless I acted quickly, so I signed the purchase contract myself – though at this stage no money had to change hands. Then I got the call – not from Bert himself, but from Darren Bradely, a bright young chap who worked for him. He told me: "We're prepared to go ahead with the development, but we don't believe there is enough profit in it to include you."

As you can imagine, this was not what I wanted to hear. I had found the site and seen the potential – they were just there to provide the backing. That was how our relationship had always worked, as Bert Perry was anything but hands on. He hardly ever saw a site himself. He was a money man rather than a property man like me – he even said to me once, "Leslie, you may be a better developer than me, but I'm a better banker than you."

The final development in Brighton, completed without my involvement

I was happy with that distinction: I was content with the work I did and proud of the buildings I erected. I never put up a factory or warehouse I couldn't imagine occupying myself. Some developers would just throw up four walls and put on a roof – and that was not for me. I always made sure the office space had attractive elevations and that the factory or warehouse walls were painted to give a pleasant finish internally. I was more than just a developer – I was a high-quality developer and always had been.

Now here I was, being shut out of a development opportunity I had found. I considered my options and decided to bow out gracefully, disposing of my interest in the site to Bert Perry and accepting that, after nearly 50 years in the property business, it was time for me to slow down and take stock.

Now I come to look back over the story of my life, I feel it would not be unreasonable to ask if I had any regrets along the way. The simple answer is, yes, on reflection there are three significant decisions in my business life that – had I made a different choice – I am convinced would have produced a far different outcome.

My main disappointment still is that I did not pay attention to the offer of funding put forward by Harry Hyams. If I had, all of my developments would have been undertaken by a single holding company without the need for external partners, as Mr Hyams had access to unlimited financial resources in the City of London. On a personal level, it is deeply regretable as he had an exceptional property brain and would have given invaluable guidance to me, as a young entrepreneur running a fast-growing concern.

My next regret is not proceeding with the merger between Estates Property Investment Company and my own Hanover St George Securities Limited when that was offered by Charles Knight. EPIC was a public company making profit and adding my developments would have produced a very sizeable concern that would have been a popular investment vehicle. Its finances would have been so solid that further success would have been more or less inevitable.

My last regret is the unnecessary and, to be honest, somewhat foolish sale of my company to the Thorn EMI Pension Fund. Effectively, I ignored my own principle of retaining income to ensure strength. Worse still, I sold out too soon to reap the full benefit, as substantial rent rises were only two-to-three years away from many tenants. While I was left with a substantial portfolio for development, that could not be done without heavy borrowing and the amount of capital made from the sale of these properties could not support future large-scale developments without risk.

Producing this narrative of my life, it is clear that I have travelled a long way – though sometimes the roads I followed were not paved. Finally, I believe it is an appropriate and nice thing to say that these recollections really did happen and became a focal part of my history.

Leslie Beaton-Brown
Newmarket, 2019

Appendicies

Leslie Beaton-Brown

Appendix i
A client list

The following companies all occupied premises constructed by the group

Aalco (Humberside) Ltd

Addressograph Multigraph Ltd

Advance Linen Services Ltd

Advance Motor Co

Armour Group

Associated British Foods Ltd

Associated Electrical Industries Ltd

Avon Rubber Co

Barclays Bank Ltd

BASF

Bass Charrington Holdings Ltd

The BBC

Beecham Group Ltd

Beeches Chocolates Ltd

Berry Magicol Ltd

Black & Decker Ltd

Booker McConnell Ltd

Boots the Chemists

Brinks Matt

British American Optical Co

British Rayphone Co

British Sidac Co

Brooke-Bond Oxo Ltd

Burroughs Machines Ltd

Carron Co

Cerebos Co Litd

Chrysler (UK) Ltd

Colgate-Palmolive Co Ltd

Courtaulds Textile Co Ltd

Dunlop Rubber Company

Elliott Machine Tools Co Ltd

Enfield Cables Co Ltd

English Electric Co

Everest Double Glazing Co Ltd

Expanded Metal Company

Fag Bearings Ltd

Fairdale Textiles Ltd

Firestone Tyre & Rubber Company

Firth Cleveland

Fishburn Printing Ink Co

Ford Motor Co

Fry Machine Tools Co Ltd

General Electric Co

Gestetner Ltd

Glaxo Group Ltd

Goodyear Tyre Co Ltd

Green King & Co

Green Shield Trading Stamps Co

Greenall Whiteley Ltd

Hahn & Kolb Ltd

Halfords Ltd

Halls Meat Co

Hawker Siddley Dynamics Ltd

Haymarket Publishing Co

Inland Revenue

International Paints Ltd

Imperial Metal Industries

Imperial Tobacco Co

ITA

Wm Jackson & Co

Jefferson Smurfit & Co

Joshua Wilson Co Ltd

Lancashire County Council

Leyland Paints Ltd

Lidl Supermarkets

Litton Business Systems Ltd

J Lyons & Co

MacFisheries Ltd

Marks & Spencer Ltd

Midland Bank Ltd

Mono-Containers Ltd

Morphey Richards Ltd

National Cash Register Co

Olympia Business Machines

Ozalid Ltd

Parke Bakeries Co Ltd

Pirelli

Plessey Co

The Post Office

Pye Telecommunications

Quinton Hazel Holdings

Radio Rentals Ltd

Rank Xerox Corporation

Ransome Marles & Pollard Lt

Reed Paper Group Ltd

Relay Exchange Co

Roneo Vickers Ltd

Rosenthal China Ltd

Wallpaper Manufacturers Co Ltd

Sealless Strapping Co

WH Smith & Co Ltd

Smiths Crisps Ltd

Sperry Rand Ltd

Spicers Ltd

Spillers Ltd

Standard Chartered Bank Ltd

Star Paper Co

Telefusion Co Ltd

Thomas Hedley & Co

Thorn Electrical Industries Ltd

Tornado Fixings Ltd

Trustee Savings Bank Ltd

Twinings Tea Co

Visionhire Ltd

Wiggins Teape

Appendix ii

A location list

New industrial and warehousing developments (undertaken directly or jointly with funding partners) and office developments.

Industrial & warehousing developments	*sq-ft*
ALTRINCHAM, Cheshire	94,000
BATH, Somerset	8000
BATHGATE, West Lothian	126,000
BIRMINGHAM (3 schemes)	58,00
BLETCHLEY, Bucks.	107,000
BOOTLE, Lancs. (5 schemes)	92,664
BRADFORD , Yorks	13,500
BRIGHTON, Sussex	28,500
BRISTOL (2 schemes)	385,000
BROXBURN, West Lothian (6 phases)	185,000
BYFLEET, Surrey (2 schemes)	97,000
CARDIFF, Wales (3 schemes)	70,000
CARLISLE, Cumbria	21,160
CHANDLERS FORD, Hants	150,000
CHELMSFORD, Essex (2 schemes)	78,000
CRAWLEY, Sussex	10,000
DERBY	45,000
DIDCOT, Berks	10,000
DURHAM CITY, County Durham	108,000
GATESHEAD, Tyne & Wear	31,000
GLASGOW, Scotland (3 schemes)	48,000
GLOUCESTER	61,000
GREATER MANCHESTER (10 schemes)	978,000
HARROGATE, Yorkshire	12,000

Industrial & warehousing developments (cont)	sq-ft
HAYDOCK, Lancs.	300,000
HINCKLEY, Leics	30,000
HULL, Humberside	70,000
LANCASTER, Lancs	24,000
LEEDS, Yorks	336,250
LLANELLY, Carmarthen	10,000
LONDON, Nl (Chrysler)	108,000
LONDON, Battersea	17,500
LONDON, Wharf Road, N1	78,500
LONDON N7 (7 schemes)	270,000
MAIDSTONE, Kent	50,000
MUNICH, Bavaria (Germany)	150,000
NEWCASTLE UNDER LYME, Staffs	10,500
NEWCASTLE UPON TYNE, Tyne & Wear	1,050,000
NOTTINGHAM	42,500
PERTH, Scotland	16,000
PETERBOROUGH, Cambs	10,800
PRESTON, Lancs. (6 schemes)	300,000
RED HILL, Surrey	10,000
ROTHERHAM, Yorks	10,000
RUGBY, Warwicks (2 schemes)	320,000
SHALFORD, Surrey	60,000
SITTINGBOURNE, Kent (4 phases)	495,000
SLOUGH, Bucks	12,000
STOKE ON TRENT, Staffs	46,000
TAMWORTH, Staffs	24,000
TEESSIDE (2 schemes)	224,000
WEMBLEY, Middx.	60,000
WESTON SUPER MARE, Somerset	3750
WORCESTER	60,000
YEOVIL, Somerset	15,000
TOTAL	**7,037,724**

New office developments	sq-ft
BIRMINGHM, Granville Street	21,000
BOLTON, Churchgate House	28,000
BOOTLE, Connaught House	10,000
BOOTLE, The Triad	250,000
BRISTOL, Kent House	6000
BRISTOL	6000
CHEAM, Station Approach	25,000
GLASGOW, Cadogan Street	13,000
GLENROTHES, Hanover Court	18,000
LEEDS, Tower House	77,000
LEICESTER, Melton Street	12,500
LIVINGSTON, Grampian Court	22,000
LONDON, Borough High Street	18,500
LONDON, Borough Road	44,000
LONDON, St. George Street	3750
MANCHESTER, Faulkner House	30,000
MANCHESTER, Princes House	25,000
MANCHESTER, Crown House	18,000
MIDDLESBOROUGH, Teesside House	50,000
NORBITON, Hanover House	18,000
NORWICH, Surrey Street	12,000
PRESTON, Guildhall Street (2 schemes)	34,000
SHEFFIELD, The Pennine Centre	440,000
SHEFFIELD, Church Street	40,000
TOLWORTH, Hanover House	8000
WITHENSHAWE, Town Centre	118,000
WREXHAM, Regent House	14,000
NOTTINGHAM, St Thomas Street	6000
TOTAL	**1,366,2500**

Appendix iii
My development projects

Images of some of my industrial, warehousing and office projects.

Oyster Lane, Byfleet, Surrey

Leighton Buzzard site acquired from Golden Ltd

English Electric Company, Tribune Trading Estate, Rugby

The Haydock Industrial Estate

Leslie Beaton-Brown

The Stanley Green Trading Estate, Cheadle Hulme, Manchester

Regent House, Wrexham, Wales

Trinity Trading Estate, Sittingbourne, Kent

Avon Tyres depot, Bristol

Phase One, speculative unit, Stanley Green Trading Estate, Cheadle Hulme

BASF, Stanley Green Trading Estate, Cheadle Hulme

Phase One, East Mains Industrial Estate, Broxburn, Scotland

Ariel view of all Broxburn phases

Leslie Beaton-Brown

New industrial units on the Haydock Industrial Estate

Development of industrial units, Essex Street, Preston

Above: Newly refurbished
office building, Borough Road,
Southwark, SE1

Left: Office for the National Cash
Register Company, Norwich

Leslie Beaton-Brown

Two office developments in Cheam, Surrey:
above, St Georges House; below, Kent House

Above: Hanover House, Norbiton, Surrey

Left: Teesside House, Middlesborough

Above and left: The Triad, Bootle

Right: Tower House, Leeds

Leslie Beaton-Brown

The Pennine Centre, Sheffield

Printed in Great Britain
by Amazon

44062807R00069